Channel Excellence

**Architect, Manage and Accelerate
Indirect Businesses**

*"Channel Excellence", provides a holistic view,
proven methodologies and innovative concepts for
channel sales & marketing people who decided to
take their respective indirect business to the next
level.*

Axel Schultze

*This book is dedicated to
the 100 Million+ sales men and
women in all kinds of indirect
channels who contribute
about 75% of the world's
revenues across all industries*

ISBN: 978-0-6151-7759-5

http://www.channelexcellence.com

Contents

Contents

The top 100 influential people to this book, channel thought leaders, channel advocates and channel experts I worked with.

I would like to express my sincere appreciation to all the contributors, who spent time in interviews or worked with me in various capacities either as employee, partner, customer or manufacturer. I was fortunate enough to work with so many smart leaders so this book could be created.

Angelika Horaitis, VP Global Channels, IBM
Beth Vanni, Director WW Partner organization, BEA
Bill Krause, former CEO, 3Com
Charlie Wallace, former Director, Hitachi Data Systems
Christian Wedell, former VP, Microsoft Europe
Christopher Clinton, Channel Manager, Citrix
Chuck Digate, Founder & former CEO, Convoq
David Dutton, Marketing Manager, Adtran
David Garcia, VP Sales, AMD
David Martinez, CEO, Infinigate
David Roberts, former VP, McAfee
Del Heles, CEO, CMR
Denise Sangster, CEO, Global Touch
Diane Krakora, CEO, Amazon Consulting
Dieter Giesbrecht, former EVP WW Sales, Symantec
Dieter Kondek, former VP Sales, Computer 2000
Dr. Juan Montermoso, President, Montermoso Associates
Dudley DeVore, VP Sales, Avocent

Duncan Potter, VP, Westcon Group
Eckard Pfeiffer, former CEO, Compaq
Ed Esber, former CEO, Ashton Tate
Elay Cohen, PRM Product Line Director . Salesforce.com
Eric Berridge, Chairman, Blue Wolf Group
Erol Kirilmaz, Dir. Partners Germany, Siemens
Evelyn Taylor, Director, SAP
Garth Olivera, Director, Sales Development, Accuvant
Gene Hellar, former CEO, Prima International
Gerd Hart, former Director Sales, Compaq
Gerd Henneveld, CEO, Hennveld
Gregg Kalman, former Director Channels, Avaya
Hans Apel, former Director Channels, Microsoft
Hans Gerke, Partner Mgr, Sun Microsystems
Harald Horgen, CEO, York Group
Heather Dawson, former Manager channel sales, IBM
Irfan Salim, former Director Channels, Lotus
Jack Rotolo, former EVP, NetObjects
Jeff Hausman, Director, Symantec
Jeremy Allaire, former CEO, Allaire
Jerry Huskins, President, Astadia
Jochen Tschunke, Co-Founder, Computer 2000
John Brandon, VP, Apple
John F. Payes former President, IAMCP
John Howard, Dir. Distribution, Avaya
John Strauss, Director, Cisco
Jost Stollman, former CEO, CompuNet
Julian Dent, Chairman, VIA
Julie Perish, Vice President Cchannels, Symantec
Karen Hartsell, Director Channel Marketing, PGP
Ken Boasso, CEO KeyChain, Logic
Kevin Jenkins, founder, Hercules Graphics Cards
Cord Behrens, CEO, IBD Honkong
Kurt Mueller, former MD, Lotus Development
Lonnie Wills, VP Services, Astadia
Marc Cooper, Director Channels, Juniper
Marco Quinter, VP Cablecom

Marita Roebkes, Founding Member Xeeque Corp
Mark Pierrett, Director Channels, Nortel
Mark Villinski, Channel Marketing Manager, Kaspersky Lab
Matt Holeran, Vice President AppExchange, Salesforce.com
Maurizio Capuzzo, VP Global Channels, Avaya
Michael Kaack, CEO Ingram Micro, Germany
Michael L. Whitener, Principal, VersaLaw LLC
Michael Poliza, former CEO< Polisoft
Michael Vizard, Senior VP, Ziff Davis
Mike Dubrall, Channel Consultant
Mike Haines, General Manager, Microsoft
Neil Isford, VP WW Sales, IBM,
Norbert Reithman, CEO, PCM
Patrick Consorti, Service Director, Blade Network Technology
Patrick McGovern, Chairman, IDC
Philippe Vincent, Partner, Accenture
Ray Norda, founder, Novell Networks
Reed Hornberger, VP Global Channels, SUN
Rich Baader, former MD, Intel PCEO Division
Robert Cohen, President, Integrated mar.com
Robert Graham, Director, NASBA
Robert Jurkowski, CEO, Selectica
Robert Wong, worldwide channels, IBM
Rod Baptie, Founder, Baptie Group
Roger Green, CEO, Ipswitch
Roger HADDAD, former CEO, Metrologie
Ron Czinski, VP WW Sales Operations, Cisco
Rudi Breiden, CEO, Unitronic
Scott Derksen, Sr. VP, IronSolutions
Scott Marshall, Vice President NA Channel Mkt., CA
Stephan Link, CEO, ComputerLinks
Stephan Rossius, VP WW Partners, SAP
Steve DeWindt, Co-Founder, BlueRoads
Steve Raymond, founder and CEO, TechData
Steven Blum, VP Americas, Autodesk
Steven Elop, former CEO, Macromedia
Subrah Ayar, CEO, WebEx

Thomas Baur, EMEA Channel Development, Autodesk
Tiffani Bova, Research Director, Gartner
Timothy Chou, former president, Oracle OnDemand
Tom Dolan, CEO, Westcon Group
Tom Valiante, VP Americas Channels, HDS
Torsten Koester, Managing Director, CMP Media
Udo Lichtenecker, Co-Founder, Computer 2000
Willy Soehngen, former VP Europe, Novell

Hundreds more I worked with in the past 25 years should be named, but it would fill a book on its own. In addition, I want to extend my sincere appreciation for all the time and support provided by Janet and Christine Diamond who helped make the content I put together a readable book.

If you like to contribute your experience, like to help others find resources or see the latest in channel development, please visit our wiki and our blog at

http://www.channelexcellence.com

Channel Relevance

I had a chance to closely work with **Compaq** Computers from start to finish. Compaq was a little startup out of Texas, founded by Rod Canion, Jim Harris and Bill Murto. I can still hear people at Comdex 1982 saying, "They [Compaq] have not even the tiniest chance to survive a competition with IBM or other giants such as DEC and Tandem". Who would have imagined that this company not only survived, but 10 years later was the global leader in personal computers? Who could imagine that a product that had not even a chance to be different but in turn needed to be "compatible" with its biggest competitor could do that? Clearly Compaq stood for quality – but were IBM's or HP's products bad? No, not at all. Was Compaq a fashion? No, that was Apple's game. But Compaq, like Microsoft, had something nobody else had: A loyal, extremely powerful indirect sales channel. At peak times, IBM and the rest of the industry had to compete with over 100,000 well trained and highly motivated Compaq resellers and it's estimated 1 million sales people in that power channel. A well structured channel of resellers, Value Added Resellers (VARs), System Integrators, Distributors and smart people within those channel companies, closely working with Compaq, were selling and installing Compaq products in businesses from banks, hospitals, mom and pop stores, private homes, to NASA, the Army and the rest of the world. Compaq was able to grow at speed of light – never was a company able to sell their products so widely spread in such a short period of time. I had several conversations with Eckard Pfeiffer before he became CEO of Compaq who was very proud on his channel. He was initially the one of the few people who understood how to leverage a sales force by managing more business through partners then managing those businesses directly. In one of the conversations he unveiled a secrete to me: " We will beat IBM by their own saying: 'All what counts is the feet on the street', when we mobilize a global indirect partner channel." By 1987 it was selling 1 Million PCs. The Compaq channel was well selected and placed to be able to sell to end consumers, small businesses, medium size companies and even global enterprises. The promise to not sell direct empowered not only every VAR to give it's best – more importantly it turned the channel sales people at Compaq into true managers, managing more business through their partner than they could ever do direct. I was often part of large deals like at Deutsche Bank, which was almost OWNED by IBM, yet the Compaq partners together with the Compaq sales force broke even in here. Like almost always, it is not the best product that wins the race for market share but the method you conquer the vast complexity of a given market. In 1998 Compaq acquired DEC and made its most fundamental mistake. Not only was dying DEC not worth the $9.6 Billion but more importantly Compaq acquired a 100% direct selling company with a global support organization that was just happy to keep a job. In 1999 the failure to migrate DEC into Compaq became so obvious that the Compaq channel became very nervous. In 2000 Compaq lost its global leadership position in just a few months. Disaster stroke at executive level. E-commerce was the hot word and direct sales ala Dell was en vogue . When Compaq announced that they will also consider selling direct, the channel turned his back on Compaq. The channel broke away in no time. Still the product was top, the quality superior, the product strategy to enforce the server business just right but the strategy just killed the single most precious asset Compaq ever had – may be without even knowing it – it's superior channel. That channel made Compaq to what it was and turned Compaq into what it would be without it – a lousy acquisition candidate in this case for HP. And again also HP executives didn't know much about channels and disaster continues.

This is even more interesting when we look into a different division of HP: The printer division. I just recently talked to Dr. Juan Montermoso a former HP manager who explained to me the enormous success around the HP LaserJet. "When we were task to sell this very expensive and unique technology we know we needed to find a specific niche to create any kind of success. We decided to sell the LaserJet into law firms because they had a high demand for quality printouts. To reach law firms around the globe it were just not economical to do that by direct sales. So the initial success was based on partners pretty much right away globally selling HP Laserjets into law firms. But the resellers very quickly found lots of other interesting use cases and customers. HP realized how fast they grew that business through its channel and made it a channel only business. In 1986 I tried to get the distribution rights for the LaserJet and had the hardest time because the whole global sales organization was fixed by one thing "Sell to resellers and to nobody else". It took 1 full year to get a contract and was finally done simply because HP was overwhelmed by reseller demand. While the greatest names in printing back then were Xerox or Epson, also here an unbelievable success by beating its competition with a totally underestimated weapon: An indirect Sales Channel.

We will later on look at other global leaders such as Microsoft, Symantec, Cisco and others who all have one thing in common: a very well architected global channel and virtually no channel conflict.

Coincidence? If we gleam just a tiny little bid into market science, it is interesting to note that Dell is the only computer company in the world who survived with an exclusive direct sales force. Like in almost all industries, the number of successful "channel only companies" outnumber the "direct only companies" by 5:1 or more. With this we will uncover a very important market dynamic: By a ratio of 5:1, more people either rather trust a local partner who helps to select the best product or just prefers the convenience of a local partner organization then there are people who insist buying directly from a manufacturer, hoping they get a "better deal".

Preface

About the Channel

There are many ways to describe a channel: resellers, dealers, VARs (value-added resellers), system integrators, catalysts, brokers, distributors, strategic alliance partners, technology alliances, influencers, and agents. Sometimes people even call direct sales a 'channel'; a direct channel. Another even more special group of channels called OEMs (original equipment manufacturer) or ISVs (independent software manufacturers), are sometimes referred to as a channel.

This book refers to channels as: "Legally independent organizations whose business model and value proposition is to "Identify, aggregate, combine, sell and service the best solutions for their respective customers". Channels, in this book, are specific organizations with value-added character that work in a long-term relationship with their respective manufacturers and are "manufacturing" themselves.

Indirect channels and its inherited challenges exist in many industries and in many forms and shapes. This book focuses on the indirect sales channels in the high tech industry, using terms and describing behavior found in traditional product sales as well as the new Software as a Service (SaaS) channel.

1. Introduction

Indirect business strategies and processes are the most underserved management aspects across all industries.

1.1   An initial set of questions

1.2   Industry trends for indirect business

1.3   Indirect business from an executive perspective

1.4   Indirect business and Wall Street

1.5   Channels, the most underestimated competitive advantage.

1.1. An initial set of questions

This first section starts with a serious of question people may have when they work in, for or in conjunction with indirect channels. Those questions are educational because sometimes one realizes there is a problem but can't articulate the cause. We will try to provide answers for all those questions in this book.

> **Synopsis**: The majority of problems can be managed by simply asking the right question. How do you develop a level of EXCELLENCE if you don't know what you don't know? National and international indirect channels are a myth to some and the most powerful sales force to others. We'll go through a series of questions in this section and find answers in the rest of the book.

The questions below are in no particular order. Some of the questions are so trivial to some and others never thought about them. There are a few which I felt are more essential then others so I put them up front.

General and often asked questions:

- How big should my channel be to reach my target market?

- How can I manage end customer satisfaction through my indirect channel?

- How can I grow market share and revenue with my channel?

- How can I ensure continuous success of my channel partners?

- What are best practices to recruit partners?

- What do I need to do to be attractive to partners?

- What should a partner bring to make me happy?

Soon more detailed questions appear:

- How can I measure my channel's performance?

- How can I measure my own performance relative to other manufacturers?

- How can I compare my channel's effectiveness with my competitor's channel?

- How can I ensure access to the market with a channel in between?

- How can I calculate an ROI on my partner marketing?

- What is my confidence level on channel-based forecasting?

- How can I plan demand with my channel partners?

- How can I manage channel conflicts between direct and indirect sales?

- How can I boost channel sales?

- How can I make my channel more profitable?

- How can I make our company more attractive for channel partners?

In order to answer those questions, even more detailed questions need to be answered:

- How smooth is the flow of sales leads through to my partners?

- What are the average sales closure rates of the partners?

- How is the lead follow-up process through the channel?

- How do partners perform relative to product lines and geographies?

- What is an average sales cycle though a channel partner?

- Which partners provide me with market share independent of their respective revenue contribution?

- How can I measure how effective the MDF and COOP-based marketing activities of my partners are?

- How can I motivate my partners to create their own opportunities and register them with me for better transparency?

- How can I integrate order processing from my channels with my own logistics and maybe even integrate distributors?

- When and why shall I engage with large or specialized distributors?

- How can I better educate my partners and improve end customer satisfaction?

- How can I build a continuous relationship between an indirect customer (a customer of my partner), the partner and my own organization, without entering into channel conflicts?

- How can I manage, track and measure results of any type of sales and marketing initiative and calculate an ROI?

- How can I expand my channel and at the same time maintain quality and manageability of a large reseller channel?

- How can I eventually leverage my channel with no additional resources but gain incremental revenue and market share?

- What partner programs worked in the past and which did not?

- What are the key requirements from a partner to engage with us as a manufacturer?

- What other questions do I need to ask, of which I'm not even aware?

1.2. Industry Trends for Indirect Business

This section discusses the trends in indirect business development, focusing on the high tech industry and financial services industries in particular.

> **Synopsis**: With about 75% of all revenue flowing through indirect business drivers, the channel has become one of the most strategic aspects in corporate development. The third millennium started with high tech consolidation and continuous growth of indirect business. Yet indirect business organizations receive the least amount of attention and credibility from management.
>
> According to the World Trade Organization (WTO) www.wto.org, about 75% of all world trade flows through indirect channels.

There are somewhere between 20 and 50 million reselling (non-producing) businesses worldwide. The sheer size classifies the challenge indirect business development is facing. Yet, no solid research is available today describing global indirect business trends and respective size information across industries on a global scale.

The computer industry has about 250,000 reselling organizations in the USA, approximately another 500,000 in Europe and another 500,000 in other continents. This totals to 1.25 million channel organizations in the information technology industry alone worldwide. In 2004, Microsoft announced that their channel consisted of 875,000 partners.

The financial services industry has about 1 million brokers and independent agencies in the USA and more than 3 million worldwide. The US car industry is composed of over 1 million resellers.

More than 50% of the 15 million US businesses are primarily resellers, dealers, brokers or distributors of goods and services in high tech, automobile, food, clothing, energy, real estate and so forth. The trend towards channels can be seen in maturing industries. The automobile industry as one of the oldest industry today sells almost everything including cars, car accessories or car services through independent dealer organizations.

Industries seem to go through a wave of direct sales, early channel engagement, channel dissatisfaction and disengagement and returning with a more mature channel. Those waves have been seen in the automobile industry, in the financial services industry, currently in the high tech industry and in many other newer industries.

Despite the economic importance of a channel for the majority of midsize companies, the channel is often the stepchild of their respective sales organization. As an adjunct to the direct sales initiatives, many sales organizations hope to get incremental revenue by "allowing" a channel partner to participate in the successes of the manufacturer. This is true in Europe and in the United States, although there are great differences in channel management and channel development between the two markets.

I had the opportunity to build and grow channels both in Europe and the US. In Europe, the channel has become the most economical and efficient way of selling almost any kind of goods, even though it is still not regarded as equal to the direct sales counterparts.

Why is the channel not equal? Since the direct sales force are the employees of the manufacturer and are therefore under the direct influence of the producer, they are considered completely loyal to the producer; whereas the channel sales force, as autonomous entities are not. Yet, both are motivated by the desire to sell and make money. The fallacy that diminishes the importance or the trustworthiness of the channel is a costly one. This book illustrates how much this fallacy costs, and how to avoid it and make your business more profitable.

First, let's explore why the efficiency driven US market actually has a harder time developing effective channels than Europe or Asia. The reason lays deep in the economic development structure of any given industry and the fact that a channel is a leverage model to support extensive demand growth – not only demand creation.

Pretty much every new product, technology or service needs at first to be sold by its creator. As long as the new solution is not proven in the market, a channel partner would not suggest it to their customers – with a few exceptions (see Definitions of Channels). Now as manufacturers gain visibility, attention and market share, channel partners may be interested in selling those new solutions. As the manufacturer still needs to sell direct as well, the conflict is obvious. At some point, the manufacturer decides to create a channel but will not take the risk to entirely trust the channel and no longer sell direct - so conflict is inevitable.

Channel partners cannot compete on price with a manufacturer in a 1:1 competition, and therefore lose interest in that manufacturer. The manufacturer, in turn, judges the channel partner's behavior as the behavior of a loser and continues to sell direct. Frequently, at this point, European users show interest in this manufacturer's solution— immediately European resellers and distributors get very active with the manufacturer. Since the US manufacturers have no representation overseas at this time, those European channels and their indirect businesses can flourish. Shortly thereafter, or in parallel, the Asian market shows interest and because of the geographic distance, the cultural differences and language barriers, the indirect model is almost a default choice.

Many manufacturers recognize the advantage of an indirect model in their P+L and try channels in the US again. Now the previous experience with channel conflicts is still present, the strong direct sales force is very active, and the switch from direct to indirect seems almost impossible. At this point, the direct sales force may be very large and even very successful. Not only it is now more difficult to switch; there is a big group of successful employees actively competing with the indirect model.

Only a few companies have ever managed to make the transition clear cut. The companies that did became widely successful: Microsoft, Symantec, Novell. Even if a company needed to go through extremely difficult times like Novell, the channel made it possible to survive.

1.3. Channels in the High Tech space

According to IDC (International Data Corporation), in 2002, for the first time in history in the high tech industry, indirect sales hit the 50% mark of revenue contribution by channels. In 2003 the information technology industry sold an estimated $700 billion worth of products through channels. With additional value added services, high tech channels in total generated about 1 trillion dollars in worldwide revenue in 2004.

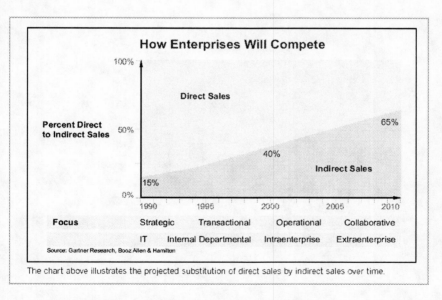

The chart above illustrates the projected substitution of direct sales by indirect sales over time.

The highly regarded Gartner research firm predicts that indirect sales in the high tech industry will contribute to 65% of all sales by year 2010.

The saying "The internet eliminates the middleman" did not become reality. The channel actually grew even during the dot com boom. The key challenge remains: How to better manage indirect business on a global scale. Many executives in Europe, in Asia and in Silicon Valley state that they want to increase channel sales. A Japanese hard drive manufacturer wants to go from 20% channel to 100%. A security manufacturer has a strategy in place to move at least 10% of business every year towards indirect, reaching 100% channel operations by 2010.

1.3.1.   Channels in the Financial Services Industry

There are similar trends in the financial services industry. More and more business is conducted through brokers and agencies. The challenge remains: How to ensure market share—and more importantly, customer retention—through those channels on a global scale.

Some of the largest financial services companies in the US and Europe are using large broker networks. Some use exclusive brokers; others, multi-channel brokers. Those networks often contribute over 50% of the manufacturers' total business. Research indicates that Washington Mutual, for instance, does 65% of their home loan business through indirect broker organizations. However, the retention rate of the direct business is about 50% greater than through their brokers. It would be easy to conclude – then do not use the channel, but that may mean somewhere between 30-60% cut in revenue. An alternative may be to better manage and service the broker network. It would be way too easy to point to the channel and declare the channel is not efficient. Information and process management through the channel becomes more important than anything else. Furthermore, with better processes, tools and information the channel will be able establish higher revenue also for retention and renewal.

Other financial services like insurance policies are sold vastly through indirect broker networks. However, it is a shocking reality that those indirectly conducted businesses are much less transparent and much harder to predict. Their business planning is more guesswork and their estimations are based on historical values rather than on indicators of market trends. The problem here is not that the indirect model is less productive, but that these businesses often use antiquated process and tools

1.4. Indirect Business from an Executive Perspective

This section discusses the responsibilities of a manufacturer executive to better manage his indirect sales contribution, the reporting thereof and the methodologies to make strategic moves and educated decisions based on a closed loop channel and indirect customer information systems. Executives on both sides (channel and manufacturer) need to collaborate closely and understand the needs and implications of the required structures and reporting.

> **Synopsis**: In order to compete on a global scale a company needs to make a decision to sell either direct or indirect. In either case a complete view of all aspects of sales needs to be developed. With 30% or more indirect sales contribution, executives can no longer be unaware of the trends and income projections from that part of their business. This information also needs to be understood by the channel-side executive to better understand the manufacturer-side needs.

As channels become a more important revenue contributor, the financial community begins to investigate a company's ability to execute with channels. As many experts in the business are aware, channels are, in many cases, a black hole. Manufacturers do not really know who their partner's customers are, what their selling methods are, on what kind of opportunities they are working and what market trends are seen between the channel and their customers.

The higher the percentage of channel revenue contribution, the stronger is the need for better management systems. However, the investor community also knows that implementing and leveraging channels is the only way to rapidly and efficiently grow a global sales presence. CEOs and CFOs are asked to better understand channels and develop sustainable channel strategies that support the overall growth plans of the company.

Channels are very complex because they are
literally outside the companies reporting,
legal and personnel influence.

Today's management information systems are not built with channels in mind. Channels are very complex because they are literally outside the companies reporting, legal and personnel influence. New systems need to be implemented to allow enterprises and their partners to collaborate in a real-time manner and provide decent benefits to the partners as well as the necessary transparency and information platform to executives. Some of those systems are introduced in the last chapter of this book.

The business world is getting more and more complex. Financial reporting regulations become more complex, products increase in variety, pressure mounts for faster operating supply chains, reliability requirements grow in complexity and sales channels grow to continuously more complex networked structures around the globe. The growing complexity requires better risk management in the financial area, better response to customer and market requirements, more sophisticated supply chains and adequate Business Networking Systems to measure model and tune alliance qualities and effectiveness.

Despite the fact that many people argue about computer-based management systems, today's world would literally come to a halt if we would take computers away, whether it is order management systems, air-travel, traffic coordination, modern surgery, space travel or simply our telephone or internet access requirements. However, there is one area -- actually a huge business segment -- that is still vastly manually interconnected: indirect business channels.

Indirect sales channels, consisting of value added resellers in the high tech industry, brokers in the financial services industry, dealerships in the automotive industry and so forth, are vastly interacting on a very manual basis with their respective partners and manufacturers. In the last 50+ years, computer applications focused on solutions that are run within a given company or enterprise and are barely connected to the outside world. Software development drove business process development and vice versa. ERP systems allow an almost seamless management of highly complex production and logistics interdependencies. CAD systems shrank product design phases dramatically. CRM systems brought a very high degree of visibility to direct sales organizations and to their customers. However, as soon as indirect channels are in place, those advantages vanish. Opportunity management, logistics processes, customer care initiatives, demand generation activities, contract renewal management, sales coverage modeling, sales lead distribution, product introductions and all the other engagements between an indirect partner channel and a manufacturer across all industries is still a vastly manual process.

"What you can measure, you can manage. What you can manage gets done." This well-known saying seems to not apply to indirect channel systems – not yet. There is no forecasting that rolls up from a partner's salesperson to their manager, to a manufacturer's regional manager and so forth up to an enterprise planning system. There is no measurement system for contract renewal rate, lead follow up rate, or opportunity closure rate. There is no measurement to track opportunity sales cycles in the channel across all partners. There is no unified deal registration and management methodology. The most complex indirect business processes are still managed manually – because of three major obstacles:

Classic data centric applications underlying the "garbage in garbage out" principle would not work. To train thousands of users from legally independent companies would be impossible. New totally intuitive and highly process-oriented applications need to be built. A "benefit model" needs to be created so that the software is not enforced but wanted by all participants.

Up until recently no technical infrastructure existed to connect all those companies on a worldwide scale. However, with the inception of the Internet managing global indirect channels is now being possible.

It has been too difficult and too complex for traditional software architecture to actually unfold a solution where tens of thousands of companies could collaborate. Even if it were technically feasible with today's software techniques, the administration of such a system would bring development to a halt. A larger partner network with 20,000 partners would involve about 250,000 users. Administration would be a nightmare. Completely new ways need to be found.

A channel side executive, running a VAR, SI or Catalyst company in turn needs to understand the reasons why manufacturer executives require more and more data. The reason is not so much the competitive nature of an industry, but the horrendous requirements of the financial market and the rules and regulations to which public companies are bound that executives require accurate, timely data. The earlier a partner organization opens up their information chest, the better it is. So it will be more and more important that the trust level between manufacturers and partners is increased and the rules of engagements are very clearly defined.

Summary: *Executives are required to incorporate indirect channels into their overall business objectives and corporate strategies and implement compensation models and measurement systems to ensure the achievements of their goals and objectives. An indirect business management and reporting system, however, can only work if a solution closes the loop with all respective constituencies. Barriers to creating data management software have fallen with the Internet. Still, the complexity of managing information from 250,000+ individuals who are not in the manufacturer's chain of command requires trust, incentives, clear rules of engagement and a very user-attractive system.*

1.5. Indirect Business and Wall Street

This section discusses the requirements the investor community will develop over time if indirect business continues to be a widely ignored aspect of management when it comes to visibility, predictability and accounting.

Synopsis: Corporations will need to invest heavily into the indirect business aspect of management. Investors will increasingly require improved methods of visibility, predictability and accounting from the companies and management into which they invest.

Today many high tech companies still sell the larger part of their US business through well-managed and rather predictable direct sales organizations. Even so most of their market, customer behavior and market trends are indication enough for investors to trust that the management team has control over sales development and market dynamics.

But as business is shifting more and more towards the indirect model, as stated earlier, many companies already sell the majority of their goods through indirect channels, the requirements grow to better understand, manage, model and tune those channels. With stronger revenue recognition rules and stronger requirements in terms of sales out reports, the investor community has already started to identify areas where they see a need to better manage a corporation's financial transactions.

Revenue recognition rules are only the beginning. More operations savvy investors are requesting a better understanding how corporate leaders predict future revenue from their channel partners. Others investigate the methods and processes of how investments into channel marketing can show a return on investment (ROI). Yet another initiative from more business savvy investors requires more transparency into how international business is conducted and, obviously, they want to understand how the company's channels on other continents compare to the competition. Even in early stage companies, wide viewing investors from the venture capital (VC) scene are very interested in understanding how their startup companies could scale up when it comes to a repeatable business process through independent channel partners. Even early stage VCs who have not been at all in favor if an indirect business model, because it is too complex and too hard to manage in an early stage company, have begun to research channel opportunities for rapid global growth.

Having a channel that sells into a large variety of market niches locally and internationally is the way to go to fast track growth. However only with the right mix of systems in place a manufacturer can accurately track business plans, revenue forecasting or marketing plans executed through a channel. Also early warning systems can only be implemented of an adequate management system is in place. Currently, indirect channel management systems are insufficiently managed when it comes to business planning, revenue forecasting, process visibility and early warning systems. To make full use of this powerful tool, corporations will need to manage indirect sales systems as well as they do their direct sales systems. For those that have mastered these systems, the payoff is huge.

However, some companies may want to avoid all aspects of channel management by continuously selling direct, however one big problem remains: How to compete if the cost of sales through indirect channels is 10% below the direct sales model and profitability is continuously declining. In the high tech industry for instance only 1 company in the top 100 firms remaining exclusively selling direct: Dell. The most successful is selling exclusively indirect: Microsoft.

Summary: Over the next 10 years, the financial community will request more visibility, predictability and accountability from the leaders across all industries. This will require better managed processes, deeper integration with their partners and systems that gauge results.

1.6.   Channels, The Most Underestimated Competitive Advantage.

This section explores strategic differences in success with companies who use channel strategies exclusively versus companies where channels are just part of a sales mix.

Synopsis: There is no substitute for a crystal clear channel only strategy. Once globally established it is almost impossible to compete. To my knowledge there is no global leader in any industry who kept a leadership for their products through a mixed sales model as long as there is a channel only or direct only player. Testimonies for that are Microsoft, Dell, Compaq, Novell, SAP, eTrade, Geico, Avon, Tupperware...

We also learned that Microsoft's channel of 875,000 partners worldwide is the largest channel in the high tech industry. Thousands of business people scratch their head wondering how this company can control the market the way they do and why it seems so hard to compete with Microsoft. I hear people saying "It is a complete myth to me that a 30 year old two product company [Windows and Office] command an industry with products that are still not stable enough to completely satisfy its users, despite of thousands of engineers. And that the very same company completely missed the Internet development, could kill a super innovative player like Netscape and after 10 years of Internet development is still behind in regards to security functionality and innovation".

Linux has been around for years. I personally heard about the final breakthrough of UNIX about 25 years ago. Although I very much admire the creation of MS Windows and Office I have to admit that I have a hard time finding a technical reason that no competitor could take substantial market share away from Microsoft. Microsoft never in their 30 year history innovated anything. They took the DOS operating system from a university in Canada, they took the Xerox invented and by Apple promoted graphical user interface, they bought companies like Visicalc and others to build their office suite and they killed Netscape in order to promote IE. So, what else is it that Microsoft has that truly nobody else on the planet has? What makes Microsoft so invincible?

The answer is so simple, yet surprising: Microsoft has the single most powerful and most effective sales force in the world: a deadly army of channel partners. Whoever wants to compete with Microsoft should not even think for 1 moment about a better product. Stop dreaming about a competing situation unless your channel strategy is 100% nailed down. It is not about the product, it is not the technology – not even a billion dollar research and development budget – it is EXCLUSIVELY the channel!

IBM created the saying: "All that counts is the feet on the street." Well – the saying does not say it must be your own team's feet. Here is my own example. How could a tiny little startup with a base capital of $15,000 (fifteen thousand dollars) called Computer 2000 in Europe bypass large hundred million dollar competitors? We did not have the capital; we did not have the product lines; we did not even have any important connections. We had only one thing: The contractually guaranteed promise to all computer resellers that we would not sell direct. This was stronger than anything our overly dominant competitors were offering. It was the guarantee of a structure, loyalty and the documented respect to what became one of the largest channels in the world, soaring to over 5 billion in revenue with over 100,000 resellers worldwide. We'll discuss some more details as we discuss the methodologies of Channel Excellence.

Now a quick journey into a completely different industry: Anchors for drywalls, bricks and other media. In the early 80's, I participated in a marketing seminar where 2 of Germany's market-leading anchor companies, Fischer and TOX, presented their sales strategies. Interestingly enough both had about 45% market share. About 25 other anchor manufacturers share the crumbs. What is so interesting? Fisher sells exclusively indirect through distribution channels. TOX sells exclusively direct. They each kept their respective market share rather constant for over 10 years. Everybody else in that business sells any way business comes in – direct and indirect, never gaining any substantial market share. The executives from Fischer and TOX respectively admitted that pretty much all the producers make quality products but only they had a very strict channel only or direct only sales strategy.

Of course, a tiny little mention must go to Dell, whose direct sales gained continuous market share and seemed the model to beat at the time. But today – we have roughly 100 computer manufacturers of all sizes on the planet – but only 1 company survived with a direct only model: DELL.

So rather than arguing over the direct versus indirect model maybe we should argue over an exclusive versus mixed sales model.

Today – 20 years later – Fischer's indirect model has one advantage: As the Chinese market opened up – they were much faster in China, and today they have over 50% market share becoming the market leader. TOX is now selling also through partners but is still mostly direct. Other manufacturers gained some market share. Fischer not only kept the German market leadership position – it is the world largest manufacturer of anchors. Fischer is still selling exclusively indirect.

All those examples show that a very strict sales strategy is more important than the discussion: direct versus indirect. If you are not a category defining company, it is hard to effectively and successfully compete on a mixed sales model. Obviously as long as pretty much all manufacturers sell in a mixed model there is no disadvantage, but if one starts selling exclusively either way it will be *much* harder to compete. As long as 50% of our profit and loss (P+L) is owned by sales and marketing line items – the way of selling and marketing is clearly one of the most influential aspects of profitability.

Another interesting company to think about is Novell. Numerous times I have heard people saying, "I just cannot believe that they [Novell] are still around".

Novell had to reinvent themselves many times. What many of us still know as the Local Area Network (LAN) leader has long ago adopted and adjusted strategies, product portfolio and services profiles. If Novell had to do that with their internal direct sales force while LAN business was dramatically declining in the 90's – the company indeed would run the risk of not being around. But like Microsoft or Compaq, Novell had one priceless force – a large and loyal global channel. Today Novell sells exclusively through channel partners, continues to innovate and today is a billion dollar company.

It will be very interesting to see how Symantec manages their sales strategy over the next few years. That company made it with $100 dollar consumer software tools such as Anti-Virus and Norton Tools Software to become a $5 billion dollar giant and the 4th largest independent software company, merging with Veritas in 2005. So far Symantec was selling exclusively through indirect channels. When one of Symantec's competitors, TrendMicro entered the security market with good products, they too were trying to develop a channel and there was great hope that they could make it with their server-based security solutions. But while Symantec continued to sell exclusively through channels, TrendMicro never made the leap to shut off their direct business. Today they sell direct and indirect, *compete within their own camp* and never captured the gigantic opportunity they had. Symantec in contrast experienced a meteoric growth and created a success story in the software industry, which was actually built on an exclusive channel strategy. Over 60,000 resellers, VARs, System Integrators and other partners suggest Symantec. If we calculate an average of 10 sales people: Symantec has a sales force of 600,000. This is very hard to compete with, even with a better product. Now, can Veritas' less strict sales structure endanger this channel sales masterpiece? Only time will tell.

With Compaq being eliminated and HP not taking the advantage they have by selling their products exclusively through partners – any computer company in the world that has a decent product would be able to compete with both Dell and HP at the same time and win the competition against both. Simply because the rest of the industry also sells in an unstructured mix of direct and indirect.

The key question everybody has to answer for themselves is: When the 1.3 million IT VARs, SIs and Resellers around the world with their estimated combined sales force of 10 million people suggest, implement and service solutions to their customers and your product is not part of the offer – can your sales force compete with 10 million local sales people in the channel?

Summary: When it comes to global market penetration: There is no economic way for ANY company to successfully outperform the existing global presence of over 1 million IT channel partners with their lower cost structure, local presence and leverage effect of combining products to complete solutions. Not even in the craziest time during the ecommerce boom did the channel take any harm. If I would run any personal computer manufacturer in the world that is producing a decent product, I would win a competition with both Dell and HP by a simple strategy: "Channel Only"

Executive Summary

The process of market and sell products and services through an indirect partner channel is more difficult than through a direct controllable sales force. Here my top 3 tips.

1)   100% direct or 100% indirect!
To run both channels and direct in parallel is like playing roulette and betting on red and black at the same time – there is no winning. I could not find a single company in any industry that was more successful with a mixed model if there is a contender with a 100% direct or 100% indirect strategy.

2)   Starting with key performance indicators!
Many managers start "reorganizing" their channel with a review of processes, methods and programs. I found that this is the single most seen mistake. I suggest the very first step is defining goals and implement ways to measure those goals – then rework your organization and structure in a way to meet those goals.

3)   Understand the strategic importance.
When you look around, in pretty much any industry, more money is wasted by messing around with indirect sales then with any other "experiment". It feels like LEARNING does not happen. If you sell through partners make it a strategic initiative, driven by the CEO.

2. Channel Blueprint

The construction of a channel organization in general

2.1.Definitions of Channels

This section defines what types of channels are broadly available, and how we usually separate the various types. It also discusses how we group channels without making it a complicated structure.

This is critically important to be able to follow the rest of this book. Most of our partnership confusion starts right here.

> **Synopsis**: Finding a balance between simplicity and well thought-out structure is one of the most over looked issues in channel development. This section puts partnerships in 3 very distinct groups: CHANNELS, INFLUENCERS and ALLIANCES.

Too often partnerships and channels are all mixed in one bucket. Whether it is a strategic alliance with a large manufacturer such as IBM, a value added reseller (VAR) such as FusionStorm or a partnership with a very influential consultant – we call it simply channel. But in order to build a robust and professional channel or partner infrastructure and ensure joint success we need to take the relationship groups apart. Only by looking at those groups of partnerships separately can we create successful plans, hire the right team, create compensation models, build our infrastructure and develop a mutually successful business relationship.

Let us first define the groups of partnerships and their respective structures:

CHANNEL is a company or individual whose business purpose and value proposition to their customers is to identify aggregate, combine, sell and service the best possible solution.

In case of the high tech industry that channel is a group of VARs, resellers, retailers, agents, catalysts, distributors, dealers or similar structures who have built a sales channel into various markets with its business purpose to represent, suggest or service specific manufacturer based solutions. A "Channel" company does not produce but presents themselves as a representative of the respective manufacturers with whom they work.

The **INFLUENCER** in turn has a very different business model and value proposition. They may as the name says "influence" a business but those companies business purpose and value proposition to their respective customers is neither to represent a manufacturer nor to 'influence". They are typically consulting companies or actually manufacturers of other products who just happen to build a symbiosis with a manufacturer and have a channel effect – but they are NOT a channel the way we define it here – they may enter into a partnership however. An influencer influences the sale of a specific product or service as a side effect of their own sales activities and their very own goals and objectives. I had several conversations with sales people and executives at BEA Inc. who were known as a thought leader in the influencer business model. But as a result they never created a robust and highly engaged channel and their direct sales initiatives often conflicted with the influencer. As a result one of the brilliantly engineered products in the Internet industry never made it to the broader market. Although it is important to understand and leverage the influencer way of doing business, it is a deadly trap to build a channel on influencers. We will discuss this in more detail a little later.

And similar to the influencer is the **ALLIANCE** partner who is not really a channel either. Alliances are often based on technology or have a marketing strategy aspect. But the business purpose and value proposition of an alliance partner to their respective customers is NOT to represent a manufacturer or recommend a manufacturer but rather opportunistically use a technology or join a sales or marketing initiative to fulfill their business mission.

Now there is still enough room to argue whether we should separate partnerships or channels this or that way. So I developed a Basic Channel Model to help understand why I made the demarcation the way I did.

2.1.1.   Basic Channel Model

What exactly is it that the manufacturer wants from a channel – regardless of what it is called? What manufacturers want is more business through others, which they cannot create for themselves. This has 3 key aspects:

- To help reach new or specific markets which the manufacturer cannot economically or structurally reach himself.

- To help grow business volume which the manufacturer cannot grow himself.

- To help provide services which the manufacturer cannot provide himself.

Those reasons contain an interesting message – the "the manufacturer cannot do himself" part. The argument is frequently put forth about whether or not a channel is of value. After all those years I conclude: If a manufacturer can do the job economically and structurally himself, that manufacturer should NOT invest in a channel. If, however, that is not the case, then truly and strategically invest in a channel.

On the other side, what is it what a partner wants from that relationship? Clearly, it depends on the category.

The CHANNEL:

- Wants to find the best products for her customers because it is not a producing entity – and will never be.

- Grows r its business with new solutions and services which it could not do without products and solutions from manufacturers.

- Creates a unique value proposition and competitive advantage by providing services only the channel can provide but no manufacturer can.

The ALLIANCE:

- Enhances its own products with other manufacturers' technology which he could not develop on his own (OEM, ISV, Development partners)

- Leverages the other manufacturers' marketing power or customer-installed base, which he does not have and cannot develop in the short term.

- Creates his unique niche position but at the same time tries to make himself independent as soon as possible to reduce the risk of getting into competition with his own partners.

The INFLUENCERS:

- Recommend a manufacturers solution in order to be able to actually have the customer execute on the suggestions the consultants provided.

Now let's review the 3 reasons to build a channel and to collaborate with a manufacturer in conjunction with the 3 types of partnerships:

1) What is the business model?

The "CHANNEL" typically has a business model that is based on reselling or referring other manufacturers' goods or services and making money by getting a product margin or referral fee. In addition, the channel makes money by implementing and servicing those solutions. Channel companies create their financial system, their company structure, their value proposition and their business relationships around that model. The value proposition certainly varies, but the overall value proposition of the channel is to help a customer find the best possible solution for that particular customer. With that overall goal the channel is per definition not the producer of that solution.

The INFLUENCER is a company that does not look at themselves as an influencer and they would deny being a channel. These consulting or technology companies have a business model based on the products and/or services they sell. The business model of a consulting firm is making money by helping their customers structure business processes, create methods, promote the customers products or services or help them with engineering, development, research or any other issue. The value proposition is typically their expertise or the solutions they sell. Those technology or consulting firms build their structure around their own solutions, their own strategies and their target customers. Influencing somebody else's business happens more by coincidence then by business strategy. The influencer's business model does not include influencing somebody else's products and receiving a fee for doing so. Calling such firms or individuals a channel is actually an insult.

The ALLIANCE Partner is very similar to the influencer from a business model point of view. But unlike the influencer whose product references are a coincidentally happening business symbiosis, alliance companies strategically work with their manufacturer partners in order to improve their business. In addition, here, the alliance partner's business model usually does not include the introduction and promotion of somebody else but rather making money by selling and servicing their own product that may be build on top or include someone else's product. In another instance, the alliance partner may push a marketing campaign that could be synergistic to another manufacturer's activities and therefore partner up. But partnering with another manufacturer will neither be expressed in the business model nor in the value proposition. However, in contrast to the influencer model the borders are blurrier.

A Salesforce.com alliance partner may actually build a product exclusively based on Salesforce.com and therefore has a business model that is depending on Salesforce.com's success and a value proposition that is built on Salesforce.com's missing functionality in a certain area. And that "missing functionality" may well be based on the fact that it makes no economic sense for the manufacturer to provide that solution himself because it is an unimportant niche. This is really the only area where an alliance partner is actually a channel for a manufacturer. However, history has also taught us how dangerous those little niches and the respective cross dependencies are for both parties.

The conclusion from the business model perspective is this: The CHANNEL has actually the most strategic connection to a manufacturer. Others may partner for a certain project or for a certain period but the CHANNEL is different in that it is a conscious, long-term, structural relationship.

When I spoke to Beth Vanni, former Director of worldwide partners at BEA, an internet application server manufacturer, it was apparent that BEA has a high focus on Influencers. However even over the long time engagement, BEA's influencer model didn't really take off and we will see little further down in this chapter what it may caused.

2) What is the channel's psychographic structure and what are the motivations underlying that structure?

Now there is a whole different set of characteristics to look at when we explore channels. What is it that each of the three groups really wants and how do they structure their teams, offerings and behavior?

Let's start with the CHANNEL again. A VAR, Reseller, Catalyst or Distributor wants to work closely with certain manufacturers and wants to recommend or sell the manufacturer's products or services because they believe in them and have a desire to tell others how good those products are.

Psychologically a CHANNEL partners with a customer – not with a manufacturer. The customer trusts that his partner will - select a different manufacturer rather than loose the customer in order to provide total customer satisfaction. The customer over time will also realize that the partner not only aligns himself with the customer but may fight for a different solution sometimes because it is a better business solution.

Like we discussed in the business model and value proposition section, the channel partner fights for a solution and can be in a unique position because he NEVER produces that solution himself.

When resellers hire, they hire people with the same objectives and philosophies: customer solution-focused rather than technology- or product-focused. The motive to select the best solution over the best deal or the preferred manufacturer is his way of thinking in business continuity. If the customer comes back because the partner provided the best solution in the first place the partner reaches profitability. One of my managing directors came from NEC and I asked him why is he interested to leave a manufacturer and join a channel organization? His answer was very determined: "I'd rather sell a solution that is a perfect match to a problem then talking a customer into a product that is just a compromise in order to get my commission".

The psychographic difference between those channels and any other player could not be bigger. Manufacturers may lose deals if they are not the best. Some of them will consider the channel partner to be disloyal because those manufacturers do not understand the opportunity they are missing to improve their products. If a channel partner would suggest a product over a competitor's product – knowing that it is the worst solution – just to be loyal, this channel partner company would soon be out of business because customers would not trust them. That kind of partner would die in loyalty.

This is all very different if we look at the INFLUENCER, the consulting and technology companies. What they really want is to consult with a customer in process optimization or technology questions. What they are proud of is their expertise, and they market that expertise. If they mention a manufacturers name just within a discussion as an example, it may have a great impact on the sales process later on. But influencing an influencer is almost impossible and even if a manufacturer were successful – she would be successful without trying because the consulting company is psychologically an expert – not a salesperson and has no interest or need to be a sales vehicle for anybody. To motivate an expert to collaborate in order to make more business is simply an example of not understanding the psychographic structure of those influencing experts.

ALLIANCE partners in this situation are closer to a channel than to influencers but again are fundamentally different than the VAR and SI type channels. Typical alliance partners are other manufacturers or service contributors who collaborate often times only during a life cycle of a product with other manufacturers. The ALLIANCE partner usually pushes its own product but collaborates with another manufacturer to increase the success rate. Like any manufacturer, the alliance partner is selling their own product and tries to do everything to be successful. They work hard to convince a customer that their—and only their—product is the best. It is no wonder that they often engage a channel partner to help sell their products into other markets or territories. Like any other manufacturer, the alliance partner is actively selling a product or service that they created and produced. The motive to collaborate is not to build a long-term customer relationship but to ensure more sales.

Conclusion: Psychographically and behaviorally, the channel has an inherent disloyalty in order to be successful. - A manufacturer has to deal with and actually leverage this disloyalty for his own benefit. But at the same time the channel has the highest degree of motivation to not only suggest the manufacturer's product but actually help market and brand it.

We have looked at the channel side of the world. Now we need to build plausibility with the manufacturer side of the world.

3) What is the best vehicle to reach the target market?

We typically think of channels because we need better ways to reach more customers. Assuming we have a clear understanding of who our target market is, we may now check and see what is the best channel to get there.

A bridge to direct sales or a long lasting relationship?

First, we need to decide whether a channel is a bridge to a market we will later on serve directly or whether we want a long lasting and growing channel relationship. Given our previous research of the business model and its psychographic structure the answer is relatively easy: If we need a long lasting trustful relationship, an alliance partner or influencer may be helpful but their business models and value propositions as well as their business motives will not convince us of a long-term relationship. Therefore, we do not need to ask questions about ability to reach a market, serviceability or anything else. Whether intentionally or intuitively most the international channels are built by robust channel partners NOT with influencers or alliances.

In contrast, if we plan to serve those markets directly but need some help, alliances with compatible products or services may create a successful synergistic partnerships. However, engaging a channel like VARs, Catalysts and others will not lead to success. In fact, it would actually delay our go to market strategy.

Conclusion: For a long-term direct sales strategy, the channel is not the right vehicle to enter new markets. However, if economically or structurally a direct sales strategy not possible, the channel is the preferred way.

4) What does a compensation model look like?

Finally the most difficult and the most uncomfortable aspect in our channel quest: How do we motivate and compensate each of those groups? The simple part of the answer: Each of the three has a different financial model:

CHANNELS receive a margin or a referral fee based on the transaction and the level of business they reached. Those companies typically have a contract with the manufacturer and clear terms or at least commonly understood rules or price lists. That margin or referral fee is an integral part of the channels' business model.

INFLUENCERS may receive some recognition, typically has no contract and it is mostly a mess to book those compensations and tracking is a nightmare for all participating parties, the manufacturer, the influencer and who ever finally caries the paper..

ALLIANCES are very different again as they mostly have predefined volume commitments which most of the times are never achieved, they have complicated cross reference contracts and even more difficult legal arrangements and part of the complication is that the type of alliance is not part of their original or long -term business model.

All three groups have one element in common: If a company is running a mixed model (direct and indirect) friction in the sales engagement and customer care increases the frustration in executing the compensation model. Typically INFLUENCERS are the most autonomous and do not really care. With ALLIANCE partners the dependency is deeper and more costly so too many partnership end with a lawsuit. The interdependency with a real CHANNEL is the deepest and therefore those relationships hold even longer. But if a manufacturer "burns" a channel – it is extremely difficult to recover.

Conclusion: Each group requires a very different and distinct compensation model in order to be successful.

I discussed the "demarcation of channels" with a business friend of mine. He was a bit surprised about me being so adamant about the clear separation and told me "You are way too religious about that – it the end we want people to sell and recommend our stuff – why do all that dissection? There is nobody who can maintain all that."

Later in the discussion, we talked about their issues with their partners, and it was very clear – partners were everything. IBM used their software in large deals like any other "OEM" software. EDS actually became experts about the respective business processes. TechData simply provided logistics. Roger, the individual consultant, helped SMB firms with the installation of the software. Every group had very different customers, strategies, motivations, and business models. The one-partner program was actually not right for any of the partners because it could not address all of the specific motivational aspects, financial models, engagements or customer needs of the respective partners.

And just recently I discussed the psychographic differences with a senior executive who admitted, "After all these years running a channel and even receiving awards for great channel management, I have to say, we made multi-million dollar mistakes and I just now understand why. How could we ignore the fact that a VAR's advantage for the customer is really being in their camp and looking for the best solution while our ISV partners push their product no different than we?"

Now, I want to state very clearly that alliance partners or influencers are very important groups of business partners for manufacturers. However, I'd like to reserve the term CHANNEL for the following group of partners: Legally independent companies or individuals whose business model and value proposition is devoted to helping customers find the best solution, yet having a close relationship with a defined set of manufacturers whose products or services collectively deliver that suggested solution.

Summary: I advocate the demarcation of business PARTNERS in the three groups of CHANNELS, ALLIANCES and INFLUENCERS. Whereas channels are companies and individuals who are collaborating in a symbiotic way with their respective manufacturers, influencers are companies or individuals who happen to help manufacturers sell their products by virtue of mentioning or recommending. Alliances are manufacturers collaborating with other manufacturers on certain specific initiatives that may be only for a certain timeframe, product or strategic engagement.

2.2. Inheriting a Channel

In this section we discuss the issues a leader faces when he inherits a channel and needs to decide how to structure the sales organization.

> **Synopsis**: The most common mistake a leader makes is reducing the channel in order to gain quality and then requesting partners to perform better. This costs revenue, grows uncertainty and brings only irritations. To develop a sound channel strategy,. a leader will succeed by embedding the channel in the overall corporate strategy and carefully planning interaction with the channel at every level.

CEOs, sales VPs and other C-level executives oftentimes inherit an indirect sales channel with no real background information why and how that channel was established in the first place. Restructuring that channel begins almost immediately. In order to get more revenue and better partners the executive shrinks the channel. He/She tries to distill more quality and improve the channel by putting more restrictions in place. This is a mistake. The result: the sales force consists of lesser partners and therefore revenue declines. All hope to pick it up later – remains hope.

There is a better way to integrate the channel into the existing organization. The first step must be a careful analysis of the channel, and what its goals are. Then the plan to achieve the goals must be reviewed and approved.

One of the first orders should be to put instruments in place that measures processes and methodologies and the corresponding results. Channel management is like many other corporate management efforts. It is an ongoing, never-ending always-improving process. You will constantly compete with other manufacturers for mindshare and provide better, smarter more attractive support to continue to have an engaged channel.

More than once, I met people who got excited about the fact that competition is everything. If a channel can compete with the direct team, the channel is good; if they cannot, it is bad. I usually try to encourage those leaders to ensure that they are consistent and structure their internal sales teams the same way: May the best win. I suggest that there should be no "named accounts", regional structure or any other territorial boundaries – may the best win and the sales people will know themselves whether it is worth flying into somebody else's territory. Obviously, I get a lot of push back. Some worry that their sales teams would leave in such chaos, others are more concerned that what would happen if everybody would undercut the prices of the other. Some were concerned about the efficiency of the team or all of the above. It did not really take a lot of time, and without me saying anything those leaders almost immediately reacted by realizing, "Oh sh...! No wonder why partners do not stay with us; Why they are not really effective. No wonder why the price erosion is happening..."

We should treat a channel like an extended global direct sales force.

Repeatedly, I see companies who view their channel partners as just another type of customer who purchase their products. I have heard people say, "Those partners are adults and they know their business, why should I care?"

I would say yes, like our employees know what they are up to when they start working for our companies and our customers who choose our products know what they are doing.

2.3.Reasons For Developing an Indirect Sales Channel

This section discusses how to determine whether a channel is a good structure for selling goods or services, and under which circumstances a channel makes sense.

> **Synopsis**: If you want to grow fast and globally, have a product in a price range below $25,000, plan to sell into multiple industries and have limited funding, you may want to select a channel as the best way to succeed.

A sales strategy (of any form and shape) should start with the market, the customers and the way to reach those customers. Then, the necessary activities to engage and close those customers will determine the type of resources needed to be successful. In addition, a key factor is the strength of the competition and the geographic reach the company wants to achieve within a specified timeframe.

An indirect channel is a good choice if ALL of the following parameters are true:

❖ If the sales process can be defined and formulated as a clear method, which can easily be communicated to sales people.

If there is an existing demand for the product or service that channel partners can fulfill based on their skills and availability to customers.

If further demand can be created on a global scale, and it is important to grow fast in order to gain and/or protect market share.

Why are resellers very economical sales channels?

Indirect sales organizations use resellers because those resellers are available around the globe. They have local access to customers, understand local ways of doing business, but most importantly, they sell 50 products at a time a when a direct sales force sells only one. This leverage of sales process energy is the only cost advantage a reseller has over a manufacturer. It is therefore very critical to leverage this effect. The more of those resellers become part of a channel, the higher the probability that additional customers are reached.

However, before going any further, ensure that you never compete with your partner; this is the golden rule for any channel initiative. No matter what program you build, no matter what incentives you introduce, no matter what discounts you offer or how perfect your product may be – **never compete with your channel**. There is not a single case where this type of competition was identified as healthy or even moderately successful.

2.4.Reasons for Developing a Direct Sales Force

This section discusses why and when a direct sales force makes more sense than indirect. It reviews potential risks in changing the sales method and looks at the advantages and differences

> **Synopsis**: If you have a product that is very support and service intensive, requires very specific project work and is over $100,000, the direct sales model may be the best to succeed.

Selling direct is the most obvious sales methodology in the early phase of a company. First, demand has yet to be created. Secondly, it is faster to sell direct than to build and to educate a channel. Third, the immediate feedback from customers is of utmost important to a young company.

If the price tag on the product is above $100,000, it is much more likely that the direct sales force remains the only sales methodology. High-ticket items typically are not very successful through a channel. Another reason for selling direct is if the target audience is a local niche market. Lastly, if a product is rather support intensive or very difficult to explain, a direct sales force may be the only way to go. Channel sales people in particular, but actually, all sales people hate complicated products – simply because most customers do not like complicated products.

Now, there is one other exception in favor of selling direct, although it is a product below $10,000, for a global market, and not complicated to sell: If the company leader just likes this model much better and sells exclusively direct. In pretty much every industry there is room for one or two such direct sales organizations. In the high tech industry, DELL is a good example. Interestingly enough, DELL is the only big PC maker selling exclusively direct. Later in the book, you will read about other examples for successful direct sales models.

A direct sales strategy is a good choice if ANY ONE of the following parameters is true:

❖ If the sales process varies by project and a lot of domain expertise is required to close a deal.

❖ If brand-new technology or solutions are introduced and demand has yet to be created. The manufacturer is happy for every business he can sign.

If the average deal size is higher than $100,000, it is not very likely that the customer will want to deal with a channel partner.

To change from direct to indirect is a big business risk. If the conversion from direct sales to indirect is not planned very well – it can cost the company.

Even so this book is about channel, there are many cases of success without channels in place. SAP for instance has a very complex set of applications that would not successfully be sold through channels. SAP has many partners who help implement and integrate the solution but not a traditional channel as we described it here. Likewise, with Siebel or PeopleSoft, both Oracle today, those products are not really channel products. It would not make sense to establish a channel just to have one.

One interesting story I'd like to share is during the time as founder and CEO of BlueRoads, a channel management software company. With all the channel experience the founding team had, we planned to sell the solution through channels. It was so obvious that a channel solution is sold through the channel that we did not even consider direct sales. We all had a great deal of expertise in corporate account sales, selling multi-million dollar solutions to fortune 500 companies.

As soon as we started to build our channel programs, we realized that several things did not really work out. Our average deal size was expected to be $50k-100k. Our focus was on the high tech industry only, and we actually focused initially only on Silicon Valley as a region. Partners were not too excited because the sales cycle was 6 month or more. We realized that what we preached before hit us without even thinking about it. Our solution was just not a channel solution even though it was the first product that really helped the channel. BlueRoads turned out to be a classic example for requiring a direct sales organization: a product in the upper price range, consultative selling, and industry specific. Now if a new company would come into the same field with a low-cost product, built for a global market and be very horizontal (useable across industries) it would be much more likely to sell through channels.

2.5. Channel Readiness

This section discusses whether or not a company is ready to develop a channel. What needs to be considered when checking readiness? The 5 key attributes to check before you engage with a channel are sales readiness, marketing readiness, product readiness, service readiness and administrative readiness.

Synopsis: Make sure you can teach anybody within 2 hours to understand your products, determine a solution scenario, price it out and understand what technical resources are required to implement the solution. Have the following things available in a documented version: Literature, pricing and discounts, order processes, technical support, return policies, upgrade policies, sales training, technical training, partner profile, partner programs, demand generation programs (leads), and sales strategy. If one is missing do not start – do not even think you can develop it later.

A product can be considered "channel-ready" when an ordinary salesperson with typical sales background understands both the need and how to satisfy that need with that product. If the education process of such salesperson takes more than 30 minutes – the product is NOT CHANNEL-READY. You may tweak it here and there, come up with special training concepts but, an indirect channel will not be the most successful model if the product is too complicated to explain. A product needs to be simple enough that the end user understands it, wants it and ideally wants the channel partner to implement it. This does not mean that a product may not be technically complex and requires technical expertise to implement and support it – but the sales process must not be complicated. I'm not saying a sales process must be short to work through a channel – many if Cisco's implementation partner go through a 6 month sales cycle to eventually get ink under a deal – but if it would be too complicated to understand what the solution is, too complicated to create a proposal, to complicated to deal with the manufacturer and ever changing price lists – the channel is not the right answer.

If the sales organization that is supporting the channel wants to be in charge of every step the resellers are doing, wants to be involved in almost every sale and discusses sales strategies, customer acquisition strategies and sales processes with their partners, that sales organization is NOT CHANNEL-READY. It would probably be more efficient, faster and maybe even more profitable to sell direct. It is imperative for a channel-ready sales organization, to leverage the channel – the more partners the better. This means that the channel-ready organization is trained and has tools and systems in place. Trending towards fewer and fewer partners that are more and more qualified is a course that will lead to sooner or later going direct or going out of business.

Moving towards a scalable channel model means growing the channel relative to demand and potential. The more partners you have, the better the market reach. A channel-ready sales organization must be able to let go. The larger the channel is the higher is the possibility for additional business.

The back office needs to be channel-ready. Announcements, communication, pricing, margin, logistics, fulfillment and all the other services need to be in place and scalable for growing or shrinking demand. In many cases, wholesale distribution is the best answer to the logistical and back office requirements of a channel-ready operation.

Finally, channel-readiness requires channel culture. Here is a channel-readiness cultural point of view: In more than 75% of the companies where I worked before I started C2000, the channel was the black sheep of the family - sort of the leftover in sales. The sales leads no one wanted went to the channel.

When a deal is won and the sales guy rings the bell, he is a hero. When a new partner is signed up – it is just another margin eater. If there is no channel culture in place, the channel adventure may become very expensive. Therefore, there MUST be a channel culture in place in order to be truly channel-ready.

One of the thought leaders in regards to "Channel Ready" in my opinion was Bill Krause, former CEO of 3Com. He ruled the company with an iron fist to ensure that the processes are in place, can be followed and simplify the interaction with 3Com. Under his leadership the pricelist became from overwhelmingly large to structured and easy to read, a product return policy was in place that if a product needed to be returned there was a simple and effective procedure everybody could follow, if new products were introduced, a product rollout plan was communicated so that we as one of their partners pretty much exactly knew what we are up against. 3Com may have not been the most sexy product but it was easy to deal with a very well operated.

2.6. Nobody Owns a Channel

This section discusses the channel partner's business model and the fact that partners need to work with multiple manufacturers in order to succeed.

Synopsis: Channel partners in the high tech industry work simultaneously with 20 manufacturers on average. If it is too complicated to work with you – 19 other manufacturers get their attention. You do not "own" your channel. You leverage an existing network of partners. As you do not "own" your employees, you need to be attractive to your partners.

Many channel organizations view their channel as groups of partners who do not do anything but sell their products. Despite the fact that such a channel partner would be soon dead. Channel marketing tends to overwhelm their partners, and based on the feedback they may receive, they return frustrated and wish they can replace their entire channel.

A channel is more efficient than a direct sales force, because the channel's sales force can sell multiple manufacturers at a time. Those resellers grow a deal, because there are 5 products from 5 manufacturers in one deal rather than having every manufacturer sell their product individually. Large system Integrators may carry products from 20 and more manufacturers. Large distributors carry 200 or more manufacturers.

A channel is a large, actually, global organism in which all manufacturers participate. The easier the manufacturer makes it for the channel partners to deal with her the more successful the relationship will be. If a manufacturer fights for mindshare and wants to engage the partner by creating complex initiatives and overwhelming requirements, the partner will soon find another manufacturer with whom it is much easier to work and MORE FUN.

One thing you will need to accept - before *developing* a channel: A business partner, reseller, VAR, or distributor -- built his success based on - providing solutions from many different manufacturers. Your business needs to be adaptable enough that a partner organization can do her job with you in a very similar fashion than she does business with other manufacturers. What you can do in order to differentiate yourself can be summarized in three areas:

- Make it extremely easy to work and deal with you.

- Provide the partner with the same attention and support that a direct sales executive would provide to his best direct sales people.

- Your product, service and mindset are channel-ready.

Today resellers are very often treated like employees in the early 18th century: It was an honor to work for a company. You had to bring your own tools in order to perform the job. You needed to make sure that you were educated and trained, otherwise you were soon fired. Every employee was an exchangeable resource; no internal development was provided. Over time more intelligent management attitudes were developed. It was understood that providing the training on behalf of the company ensured that everybody had the same level of education. It was soon understood that providing tools attracted more employees. Attracting motivated employees provided better results. In the 3rd millennium this will be a similar trend for channel partners – where PARTNERSHIP is the headline of the engagement.

Summary: It is pretty important to understand that a partner needs to handle many manufacturers and many product lines in order to achieve profitability through efficient sales engagements with many manufacturers. Being the preferred manufacturer is obviously a goal, being the only manufacturer would be negative. Manufacturer and channel live in symbiosis.

2.7.The Core Strength of an Indirect Channel

This section discusses the strength elements of an indirect channel. It also reviews a typical expectation from a typical manufacturer and looks at how this picture may need some realignment.

Synopsis: A channel is NOT a marketing organization but a pure demand fulfilling/selling machine. Like 75% of the world's sales activities, a channel is selling into the installed base (simply because demand drives a customer back to its known supplier). Hoping that a channel creates demand, creates a market, or identifies new customers is one of the biggest misunderstandings of the channel's core strength.

In 90% of the cases, the core strength of a channel and its respective partners is seen totally differently from the manufacturer's point of view than it is from the partner's point of view. Now partners believe they know what the manufacturer wants and present exactly that picture – the disaster is programmed.

2.7.1.   The Manufacturer's Point of View

Manufacturers hope that channel partners market and sell their products in the partners existing territory and to their existing customer base. That translates to incremental revenue and hassle-free sales. In the end, the partner pays in time, takes care of the problems with the customer, and handles all the implementation and delivery. Since the partner "wants" to resell the product, he will need to send his people to training and pay for the training to show at least "some commitment". In order to protect the price, the profit the margin should be minimal in the first 6 months.

2.7.2.   The Partner's Point of View

Resellers and VARs hope that the manufacturer is a strong marketer has a solid product and an existing customer base so the sales process is proven, the product is bug free and the demand drives inquiries and prospects to the reseller. With extended payment terms from the manufacturer he is able to live off of a smaller margin, and can therefore compete with the rest of the world and sell his services. Since the manufacturer wants him to resell the product, the manufacturer should pay for the training, pay for the initial marketing campaign and provide an extra discount in the first 6 months, since his sales people would not see an incentive to sell something new where the commission is not ensured yet.

Clearly, this is a typical 180-degree model: Expectations are exactly contradictory to each other. You may say, "Why have a channel, I can do that on my own." The answer is equally simple. You are right. If you can do it on your own, do not engage a channel. It will be a disappointment on both sides. However, if the demand you create is global and widely dispersed across countries, and you cannot afford to sell a $500 product directly because your salesperson is too expensive– consider engaging a partner network to fulfill the demand locally and worldwide.

2.8. Twenty Golden Rules for a Successful Channel Development

This section gives a high level overview of the most important best practices rules to make a channel successful

> **Synopsis**: A channel will only be successful if it is embedded into the very corporate strategy, with CEO sponsorship and the respective planning including sizing, profiling, and product and operational backend readiness. Preventing channel conflicts and setting up a clean and clear compensation pricing and margin model is as important as a well thought out demand creation and support program.

1)   Executive sponsorship

To make a channel successful, the top executives need to decide that the channel will be the strategic sales force of choice. Otherwise, the channel will remain the stepchild of the corporate family and a costly and frustrating undertaking. Without the CEO's total commitment, no channel will ever be successful.

2) Size your channel

Identify your total available market; assume your channel partner will have 50 active customers on average at any given point in time. Apply the 80/20 rule for your active partners and calculate your channel size by having a tenth of the number of target customers as the number of partners you need to succeed.

3) Ensure channel readiness

Make sure you can teach anybody within 2 hours to understand your product, configure a solution, price it out and understand what technical resources are required to implement the solution. Have the following things available in writing: Literature, pricing and discounts, order processes, technical support, return policies, upgrade policies, sales training, technical training, partner profile, partner programs, demand generation programs (leads), sales strategy. If one is missing do not start.

4) Think leverage

A channel is supposed to be a leverage model. If your sales people can manage 10 opportunities at a time, expect your channel to do the same and your sales people to manage 10 partners. Now your team is managing 100 opportunities at a time. Don't expect less unless there is no market – and then there is no channel.

5)   Never compete with your channel

No matter what programs you create, no matter what incentives you introduce, no matter what discounts you offer or how perfect your product may be – never compete with your channel. There is not a single case known where this type of competition was identified as "healthy" or even moderately successful. If you need to be challenged – challenge your direct competitor, not your partner.

6)   Never expect your channel to create demand

A channel is the extension of your sales initiative – not an extension of your marketing organization. You create demand – the channel identifies, fulfills and supports the demand. Channels do not own the brand; you do. Channel partners rely on your leads to open new opportunities.

7)   Recognize that you do not own a channel

There is no private channel. Manufacturers participate in a global organism called channel. Channel partners can only be effective and successful if they provide an adequate selection of manufacturers and products to market (their and your customers). Partners need to work with many manufacturers to be respected and successful.

8)   Make it easy to work with you

It is obvious yet it is the most ignored topic: Making it easy to work with you. Channel partners do not want to waste their time with administrative overhead and complicated programs, pricing models or service requirements. Channel partners are sales organizations whose foremost goal is to sell. If it is complicated to work with you, you will lose mindshare no matter how attractive your product or margin is.

9) Make margins or referral fees part of your cost model

Do not argue about the margins your partners should or should not have. Once you calculate the cost of your own sales and what your cost of sales needs to be, provide this as margin to your partners. If you can sell it cheaper – do not engage a channel. If you cannot engage a channel, if you cannot make a channel profitable, discontinue the product. Do not calculate what the lowest possible margin is you have to give but what the margin needs to be for your partners to generate a profit out of your business.

10) Introduce Systematic Reporting and Communication

One of the most frequently heard complaints about partner performance is their lack of reporting and planning. However, in almost all those cases there is not even a suggestion about how the partner shall report, to whom she shall report, in what cycles the reports are needed, what the content should cover and, most importantly, what the manufacturer does with those reports. Keep in mind that a partner will need to report to 20 or more manufacturers every month. Make sure that the reports are reduced to the smallest simplest form possible. After all that I've seen, I believe the most valuable investment is a robust reporting system. .

11) Provide basic training for free

What you do not expect from your employees, do not expect from your partners. It is in your best interest to provide the training *necessary* to sell your products. Partners will need to invest in time and resources, that is enough. Always request sales training if a product requires education to sell it effectively, just like you would train your own team. Do not make training a "sign of commitment".

12) Have *compelling* partner programs in place

The high tech industry has about 500,000 reselling organizations of any kind in the US alone. Over 5 million companies, groups or individuals are reselling or influencing sales. You need to attract partners and constantly engage, motivate and reward them. You need to be attractive, profitable and fun to work with. To partners this is more important than to be the world leader in your space.

13) Have your back office channel enabled

Your internal channel team needs to be intimately familiar with your pricing and discount structure, channel authorization processes, credit checks, logistics, return policies, MDF & Coop programs as well as customer calls from your "Indirect Customers", the customer of your partner.

14) Crystal clear regional management

Nothing is more confusing for a channel partner than the territory definitions of their respective manufacturers. overlay organization, multiple layers of responsibility, overlaps with direct sales and the constant changes within these structures makes it *very* hard for partners to develop a relationship and find immediate go-to points when sales support from the manufacturer is needed. Needless to say, even the manufacturer-side internal sales teams are often confused with territorial responsibilities, overlapping areas and confusing rules. Make your territorial definitions simple and clear so they fit on less than one page and include a map of the regions.

15) Have a channel-aware compensation model in place

Too many times partner managers on the manufacturer side have no efficient bonus plan in place and end up being more a partner administrator than anything else. Compensate your channel sales people on sales out reports from their respective partners and on per partner achievements against forecasts and plans. Modern channel management solutions are powerful enough to break revenue down to the deal level.

16) Have crystal clear recruiting and profiling rules

Have a very clearly defined profile of what type of partners you need and how many you need (see sizing). Recruit partners only against the profile or adjust the profile. Do not frustrate partners and your own team with partners that do not match. Define very clear recruiting goals and compensate your team based on successes against the plan. It is a good behavior to let the existing and new partners know what your goals are.

17) Have a well defined service business strategy

Define who provides which service. There may be services that the manufacturer is required or strategically interested in providing. Others may be necessary or desirable to be provided through the channel. A good practice is to develop a service map with clear demarcation of who is supposed to provide what service to whom. This is of utmost importance when dealing with influencers or SaaS catalysts.

18) Define the reason for your channel

Define (at least for yourself) why you want a channel and what advantage you see by having a channel in place. Define what type of investment you want to make in your channel and whether your channel has the highest priority or a secondary priority relative to direct sales. Let your partners know.

19) Clearly define and communicate your channel strategy

Define what role the channel plays in the overall corporate goal and the strategic objectives for using the channel to reach your goals. When you think of a channel strategy, do not think of a strategy to get a channel, but what strategic roles your channel needs to play to achieve your corporate goals.

20)   Be realistic

If you or any of your executives believe that your direct sales organization is better or more efficient than a channel – discontinue your channel program and sell direct. Corporations waste more money and time in trial and error on indirect business than on any other business experiment. If your company is not ready to do a full-fledged and strategic channel approach, do not even try.

There is a long list of other topics to consider such as MDF and Coop programs, RMA process definitions, pricing definitions, product packaging, partner portals and many others which also may vary by business model, product types etc. The above 20 Golden Rules however have proven to be valid and fundamental for a successful channel across manufacturers and channel types, across industries and across continents.

Summary: Take a channel as serious as having a child. Once you burned a channel it is very hard to recover. Multi-billion dollar companies, who want to recreate a channel after some missteps, have suffered for years and have needed to spend tens of millions and even more time to recover trust and engagement. If I had to pick one single topic to focus on – I pick the reporting system.

Executive Summary

Do it right at the first time. Here are my top 3 tips.

1)   Ensure that the channel strategy is a CEO topic!
If a channel strategy is something a midlevel manager has to decide and to manage, it is like employees don't count in the mind of the CEO. Nobody can expect a partner to bed his business and develop loyalty if partners are just a nice to have add-on.

2)   Ensure Integration.
Driving business through partners means not only sales alignment but every aspect of the company need to be aligned: Support, finance, logistics, production, product development, training, marketing, services and operations. Most channels fail because it is seen as a reselling customer.

3)   Understand the partner
Within every partner working sales, support, marketing and operations people. Every partner has a legally independent entrepreneur who decided to builds a business by reselling other peoples products and services – leveraging and appreciating those organizations is the whole grail of a an excellent channel organization.

3. Methodologies for Channel Excellence

Disruptive methods for channel excellence

3.1. Overview

The following chapters describe the most important process elements and methodologies we developed to improve the processes and gain better effectiveness and higher sales results. Again, the "we" is the teams I had in my 20 years of working with channels in Computer 2000, Infinigate, BlueRoads and lately in Xeequa. In order to be able to measure the success of the processes and being able to further refine the processes, we develop systems that allowed us to collect key performance indicators so we could actually measure results in a repeating model. In order to architect, manage and accelerate a channel to excellence – the most important thing is developing a way to measure success and get homogeneous reports.

As the old saying goes: What you can measure you can manage, and what you can manage you can get done.

This section discusses the background for the channel excellence methodologies and the reasons for developing them.

> **Synopsis:** With 20 years of channel domain expertise, I realized that the biggest issues with all channels occur through misunderstanding. Most misunderstandings occur due to lack of measurements and reporting. Rather than developing yet another loyalty program or a better discount structure we need to completely overhaul our business processes and put methodologies in place that reflect the best practices in the channel as well as disruptive methods that do not put bandages on broken processes. In order to measure success – we need reporting systems that did not exist yesterday.

Simply renewing channel processes and structures requires diving deep into the existing ways partners conduct their business and identifying broken links in the manufacturer-partner relationship. It also requires fully understanding the motives of business partners and their people as well as the business and process needs on the manufacturer side. To complete the picture, it requires integrating distribution models and other alliance aspects that are vital to the sales and marketing processes. A holistic view of indirect business structures that incorporate the entire industry needs to be drawn. A manufacturer is not the only player within a distributor's or a reseller's purview and not even at the customer front. The channel methodologies need to incorporate all manufacturers, their cross-networked partners and channels as well as the widely incorporated solution deals at the end customer location.

In order to comprehend the magnitude of the project we took a bird's eye view and zoomed from a global perspective down to an individual object in the structure. We looked at the various manufacturers who use a variety of distributors, who sell through their respective resellers who in turn sell to the end customer. We also took into account that, based on cultural differences such as seen in Asia, the chain may be even deeper with more layers.

We identified four key topics that are also the most controversially discussed aspects of channel management: Leads, Margins/Compensation, Training and Channel Conflict.

3.1.1. Four Key Channel Topics: Leads, Margin/Compensation, Training and Channel Conflicts

This section discusses the key needs and expectations partners have from their manufacturers. Most manufacturers have a very different view of what partners "suppose to need".

Synopsis: Sales leads, better margins and more free training are the most request items from channel partners. Channel management needs to address those 3 topics right away. Provide hot leads to ALL partners, calculate a decent margin and compare the offer with your competitors, provide basic training for free and incorporate constant knowledge transfer to the partner's sales people. But all this is immediately overshadowed by channel conflict if a manufacturer competes with their partners.

For over 10 years, channel studies and surveys have been asking, "What are the most important items you need from your manufacturers to be more successful?" The 3 line items topping the list of requirements have been: Leads, Margin and Training.

All three topics repeatedly create great debates and controversial discussions. Those three are not even discussed if Channel Conflict is on the list.

Partners want more leads. Manufacturers want feedback that is more precise. Some partners do not get leads at all – other partners do not want leads at all. In the end the return on leads is questionable, the processes are invisible and the frustration level is continuously reaching 100 out of 100 points.

Partners want more margins. Manufacturers want a more stable pricing. Some partners drive the street price down to almost cost, while others need greater margin to better market and support the products. Manufacturers compare a product margin for partners with the tip a hairdresser gets, others are very generous because they know that their own sales force can even undercut those prices.

Training is often a nice revenue stream for manufacturers from their channels. Partners invest and expect a return. This may be in synchronization but maybe not. Other partners see themselves as the extension of the manufacturer's sales force and argue that their own sales people do not pay for the training either.

Each of the topics has deep roots into the channel strategy and clearly needs to be discussed in detail. The more we dive into those three requirements and the better we understand the operation of a reseller, the clearer it gets how important those are.

As I speak with manufacturers I often hear their view of the partner's needs and what the partner "should require". I hear things like: They should require their own sales people to get - more training (which we offer). They should require us to provide financial services like leasing (which we provide). They should require more from our marketing material (which we offer). They should...

I rather listen to what the partners are saying and trust that as long as they have a healthy company, they know what they need.

3.1.2.   Partner Integration

This section discusses ways to deeply integrate partners into the manufacturer's business, from sales and marketing to product development and reporting.

> **Synopsis**: Professional system integrators, VARs and catalysts enjoy partner programs, promotions and loyalty initiatives – but that does not help bond a deeper and long-term partnership. But as partners become not only informed but integrated in the company's strategy, sales plans, product roadmap and become an integral part of the company's long-term plans, loyalty grows and equally does the performance and level of engagement.

Partner organizations are companies with their own leadership, their own P+L and their very own business strategy. And as we explored in the first chapter of the book – channel partners such as Sis, VARs, catalysts, resellers and similar organizations are dependent on the manufacturer's ability to collaborate. No loyalty program in the world can even touch the power of a deeper strategic engagement where partners and manufacturers know about each other's strategies and development plans. The more openly a manufacturer communicates the more the partner respects confidentiality. Developing that level of trust takes time of course. But the shorter that time line the faster the manufacturer is successful with their partners. Likewise, it takes time for a partner to open up when a new manufacturer comes into their portfolio.

Developing a high level of trust is only the beginning. Hopefully, that trust is now fulfilled by more extensive reporting and sales intelligence to enable both parties to accelerate their learning and improve the way they do business with each other. Knowing the trends in the local customer community is one thing, but knowing the sales people's performance, average sales cycles, latency from lead identification to opportunity engagement down to the actual results measurement provides manufacturers with the planning data to improve their business. Furthermore, It allows the channel to provide feedback, benchmark data to the partner to improve their business.

Most of the channel organizations today measure their partner's performance by the revenue they contribute. Very little is known about the partner's internal sales processes and ways of motivating and compensating their sales people. The reason for such lack of information lies in the variety of channels, the fact that they are legally independent organizations, but foremost because no reporting tools are in place that easily allow a manufacturer to receive consolidated and homogeneous reports. The single biggest problem in today's super-connected and highly informed world is that the business between partners is in many regards manual and more antiquated than most manufacturer/customer e-business relationships. To architect, manage and accelerate indirect business, the most needed instrument is a joint reporting system.

While most manufacturers just through their leads over the fence, best practices show that once the manufacturer sales people truly "share" the leads with the partners, the sales engagement process changes dramatically from finger pointing to collaboration. Systems to actually support that behavior are rare. One of the systems is created by BlueRoads that introduced a very innovative technology called APN (Active Partner Networking). It didn't quite allow partners and manufacturers to collaborate over an opportunity, but was an important step towards collaboration. Another system is Xeequa, where manufacturers and partners can truly collaborate over opportunities where even multiple partners can work with others on one and the same opportunity. We will explore those systems in more detail later on.

3.2. Methodologies for Channel Creation & Recruiting

How to create a channel and successfully recruit partners to compete in the market and grow market share

3.2.1   Channel Strategy

3.2.2   Channel Sizing

3.2.3   Partner Profiling

3.2.4   Channel Creation

3.2.5   Building a SaaS Channel

3.2.6   Partner Recruiting

3.2.7   Channel Conflicts

3.2.1.   Channel Strategy

This section discusses how to start building a Channel Strategy and get the strategy incorporated in the very fabric of an overall business strategy.

> **Synopsis**: Identifying reasons to build a channel, creating a sales, marketing and support strategy and getting buy in from the CEO (even if it is a multi-billion dollar global enterprise). Developing the main strategy framework.

The final channel strategy document will have a bit of everything we will discuss in the following chapters.

Developing a channel strategy for a company is a complex and challenging task. It is very important to understand who is the initiator of the channel development, who are the approvers and how it will be incorporated in the overall sales strategy. Indirect channels are not just mechanisms to implement – they consist of hundreds and thousands of legally independent companies with their very own leadership, their strategies, business goals and financial planning. There are best practices for leveraging those channels without the need to interview ever possible partner on the planet.

Like every other strategic plan also the channel strategy should be built based on a framework. I used the following structure over and over again, with constant fine tuning of course. This 10 topic channel strategy should work for most indirect channel operations:

Top 10 Questions a channel strategy should answer:

- Why are we building an indirect sales channel and how does that fit into our corporate strategy?

- How do we demarcate direct from indirect business and how do we transition from one model to the other?

- What is our expectation from the channel, how big does it need to be and what are the key qualities?

- What do we need to invest in order to build the channel and where does the investment come from?

- What are the underlying assumptions in terms of state of the industry, customer and buying trends, our own organization?

- What products do we sell through the channel and what does a partner need to do in order to effectively and successfully sell those products?

- How do we support the channel partners and how does that differ from our current support methodologies?

- How do we support partners with demand creation and demand fulfillment?

- What kind of margins or fees do we provide our partners and how do they differ from our current cost of sales model?

- How do we plan, get reports and be able to manage the indirect business?

Each of the 10 topics should have an executive style answer, resources assigned, budgets defined, explicit time lines and measurable goals as well as the necessary milestones. Each topic should have a very clear description about how the company is planning to conduct the tasks.

It is a good practice to let the team work closely together with the first possible channel partners to identify any obstacles or misunderstandings early on. Also, the earlier partners are involved the more likely it is that partners will buy in into the new channel strategy later on. I have used Advisory Boards early on with great success.

In 1986 we developed the Computer 2000 PowerCenters, where we expected partners to represent our company across all product lines. Furthermore, they could only become a PowerCenter if they agreed to represent all product lines. Fortunately we discussed this requirement with our elite partners being pretty confident they would like the status and the recognition. To our surprise, they explained that there are always certain focus areas so that they just cannot successfully sell the whole range. Some partners were extremely successful in the corporate business but just would not want to sell lower end products into the SOHO market. Others were very successful in the health care industry but due to federal regulations could not deal with certain other products. Fortunately, we discovered these concerns early enough to build target market specific centers – very much appreciated not only by the partners but even by the end customers.

In 1996, we discussed distribution across Europe for a manufacturer. The manufacturer, however, requested a $30,000 initial order, otherwise he wanted to setup a multi-distribution channel across Europe. We encouraged the manufacturer to do that since we would not agree to such an order. It was all about the investment strategy into a channel or geography. That manufacturer just did not do his homework. For us, it was not about a $30,000 order, it was about the lack of financial planning before entering a specific territory, such as Europe. The company needed 6 more months to actually figure out what they wanted. The product was excellent, but the company was very inexperienced. Nine months later a new manufacturer appeared on the horizon. The product was not as sleek but the company had a robust plan and a very clear channel strategy in place. Just 6 months later that company, Allaire, had distribution across Europe and became a clear market leader in Web Application Servers.

3.2.2.   Channel Sizing

This section discusses how to effectively decide how big a channel should be.

> **Synopsis:** Identify your total available market, assume your channel partner has 50 active customers on average at any given point in time. Apply the 80/20 rule for your active partners and calculate your channel size by having a tenth of the number of customers as the number of partners you need to have in your partner circle.

One of the best-kept secrets around channel development is sizing. There are companies with about 200,000 partners others with 800,000 and again others with 1,000 or 60 partners. The spread is so big that quality does not seem to be the only differentiator. Microsoft has about 800,000 partners, IBM about 90,000 partners, Cisco about 30,000 partners.

Some companies try to reduce their channel in order to get the highest possible quality. Is that the right thing to do?

Others grow their channel size in order to leverage every partner out there. Is that the right thing to do?

Some keep the number of partners small, because it is the only way to manage all the partners with a small team.

Others see channels as a huge leverage model and do not worry about a too big a channel. Is there a formula?

Yes, there is. Very large distribution organizations with hundreds of thousands of partners and very successful large manufacturers with their successful channel developed great recipes - always kept highly confidential. "What counts in sales are the feet on the street."

3.2.2.1 The Seven Most Important Elements of Channel Sizing

1) Market Size Analysis

Before you ask yourself how big your channel should be and how many partners you want or can handle, find out how big your total available market is--not so much from the revenue perspective, but from a number of companies or consumer perspective. If your market (not your current or targeted market share) is 5,000 companies in the US you may need 100 partners to reach that market - not to mention to successfully sell to that market.

If you are after the mid-market with about 600,000 companies in the US you may need 12,000 partners to just *address* this market. If you go after the Small Office/Home Office market with about 3 million organizations, you may need to have 60,000 partners to address that market. This assumes that a partner has about 50 active customers at any given time. Now, since there is a great deal of overlap the numbers can easily be doubled to really REACH OUT to that market. So trying to address the mid-market with a few hundred partners does not get you anywhere - even with the best of best VARs you can imagine. The rule: Figure out how many companies you want to sell your product to in order to find the right size channel. Get this number for the USA, Americas, EMEA and APAC.

2) Industry Differentiation

Once you have a basic idea of the number of companies you are addressing, you may need to review how they are spread across industries. Either you want to cover all industries or you only want to cover specific industries. Make that decision and keep it very clear because this will influence your channel size and profile. If you address specific industries, it is much harder to size your channel, because most of the partners do not differentiate their customers by industry. If you address an industry, simply double the number of partners you would calculate to ensure you get the right coverage.

3) Partner Engagement

Usually, only a small part of the channel is highly engaged. The good old 80/20 rule fits the channel model as well. 20% of the partners are highly engaged and bring 80% of the revenue. The other 80% of the partners seem less important and bring in only 20% of the revenue - but they contribute to market share as well. Remember it is not only the revenue per partner that brings market coverage - especially in the mid-market - but also accessibility to customers in a given market or industry. Another aspect of engagement is that partners that are smaller simply cannot take on more business but need to complete a project with the resources they have. Partner engagement varies over time. Terminating momentarily less engaged partners might be a big mistake. Even so 50 customers per partner may be a good average - to reach an entire market, it is a good rule to cut the number in half. Assume 25 active customers per partner to reach out to your target market.

4) Competition Factor

Your competition may have a larger channel. Creating a product with more quality may not help you conquer your competition. What counts is the accessibility to the target market - with channels in place you not only compete against your direct competitor but against every single partner out there.

Also here: Size Matters. The channel size of your competition should not affect the number of partners you calculate for your right size, but it may be a good mark to calibrate against.

5) Channel Management Psychology

By far the biggest obstacle to growing large channels is the fear that you will have too many partners to support. Well if all those partners are active and request support, I would say what a great problem to have. Every successful large channel organization seems to have far too many partners. The limitation of a channel is driven by channel managers who developed the rule that you cannot manage more than 25 partners. I say that this is wrong: You may not be able to manage more than 25 active partners, but the partners are usually not always active at once.

Suggestion: Group your partners in 3 categories: Highly active, sporadically active and infrequently active. Have one manager manage about 30 of the highly active partners. Other managers may manage about 100 sporadic active partners and have someone manage about 250 infrequently active partners. For a 20,000 partner network with 10% highly active, 20% sporadic active and 70% infrequently active partners you need about 70 plus 40 plus 60 people and maybe another 30 top account managers who manage the top partners on a 1:1 basis. Two hundred people for 20,000 partners is a good and efficient ratio.

6) Executive Strategy

Defining the size of a channel is a decision the CEO together with the VP of sales has to make. The channel size goes hand in hand with decisions like which market to address, how to go to market, how to market, what products to build and what service is required to support the products. If the CEO does not support the channel size a channel usually remains crippled and has no real chance to be successful, simply because this is a very important decision. Clearly over-distribution is a concern. – However, it takes a lot to actually over-distribute a market. Right sizing must be the bigger concern.

7) The Final Math

For the MidMarket

If you are going after the mid-market on a global scale and you are trying to reach more all industries, you need around

120,000 partners to simply have access to that market. With about 3 million companies worldwide that have more than 50 employees and "decent" revenue (decent varies by country) and taking about 25 active customers per company into account, you will end up growing your channel to approximately 120,000 active partners. Initially you may need to address your channel development initiative to about 1 million VARs and resellers globally to end up with about 120,000 partners.

For the Global 5,000

If you are going after the global 5,000 companies, you may need around 200 active partners. However, since those are highly specialized partners, they are harder to find and to develop.

For the SOHO Market

If you are going after the SOHO market, you will not only need retail but all the little resellers and dealers to reach you entire market. With about 3MM plus US SOHO businesses and about 20MM+ worldwide, you need about 800,000 partners to address this market. The fact that Microsoft has 800,000 partners is no coincidence.

The above formula brings you only to market reach not to market share. If the 80/20 rule applies to your channel, you may have a chance to grow to 20% market share. If your commitment is to grow 120,000 partners, you can reach out to the mid-market. With 120 partners, you can reach .02% market share. If you chose to sell direct you will need the same model to be successful, but you will compete against about 500,000 US resellers and 5 million worldwide.

Channel Excellence Methodology *suggests that you develop a clear data framework from your total addressable market by geographic region and by product family. Apply the respective calculation and define the size the channel should have in each territory and for each product family. You may get even more granular by applying this to certain verticals or customer groups like small, mid-market and enterprise. Store these target data in a system and recruit a channel that matches with those goals. This way the channel should be neither over-distributed nor underserved. The respective channel representatives in your organization should have clear objectives and a good understanding of that process.*

3.2.3. Partner Profiling.

This section discusses how to develop an ideal partner profile. What are the most important attributes of a partner representing the manufacturer? This section also discusses market access, technical ability, sales ability, current structures and potential for growth.

3.2.3.1 Dynamic Partner Profiling

This section discusses how we can get on top of the typical contact data and after-the-fact revenue information, as well as additional performance and behavior patterns that drive a dynamic partner profile, show development and allow management of partners in real time.

Synopsis: Like customer profiling in direct sales, partner profiling is one of the key activities used to structure sales efforts. But compared to customer profiling, partner profiling adds an additional level of complexity: The maintenance of the data is a big issue. Structures in a partner network are changing quickly, and the partners in this leveraged model are not managed by a dedicated sales manager. In addition, developing a partner network is more like developing a sales force than developing a customer. Performance indicators are much more critical in the pre-revenue phase and therefore, need close monitoring. This monitoring is unique to partners, and we call it dynamic profiling.

Two things are absolutely mandatory in professional and robust channel profile management: **Data maintainability** and **real-time activity and results profiling**.

In order to develop a profiling schema it is important to determine the business-relevant aspects of these profiles. We identified market and solution coverage as the two most important elements next to sales strategy and financial health. Both aspects have a static and a dynamic component: The current sales organization of the partner and the dynamically changing activity and success pattern of that profile.

A powerful profiling system has to cover the static as well as the dynamic profiling elements and needs to be self-administered by the partner as well as have automatic profiling updates by the system itself.

3.2.3.2   Partner Profiling Aspects

Partner profiling is similar to most customer profiling activities. Once a profiling initiative starts, the profiles develop quickly and a company has a good overview of their customer base. Over time, the information erodes and the day to day fight of sales people with their CRM systems begins. An almost identical problem happens with business partners such as resellers, VARs, system integrators or distributors. But one big difference makes it even harder: The channel is implemented as a leverage model. Not every partner is managed as closely as a direct customer. Data maintenance quickly becomes next to impossible.

The quality of a profile is more than just names and historic revenue. Much more important is information that helps decide campaigns, programs, support activities, marketing initiatives and more. This information is not historic revenue data, but other data such as sales initiatives, customer contact frequency, closure rates, geographic demand fulfillment, gain in local market share and similar data.

Two things are absolutely mandatory in professional and robust channel profile management: **Data maintainability** and **real-time activity and results development**.

To achieve these goals, imaginative thinking is required. Our finding is that the only way to maintain data and status from a larger channel is a channel-side self-administered system. The author invented a disruptive new technology called GNA (Genetically Networked Architecture), a unique yet simple to use architecture to ensure data accuracy. After over 20 years of channel management experience I discovered the following 4 attributes are most important to partner profiling: Solution Coverage, Market Coverage, Sales Strategy and Financial Health. Within solution coverage, questions regarding training and project handling capabilities need to be included. Likewise, in market coverage, geographic or industry specific elements need to be included.

3.2.3.3   Partner Profiling Today

Currently most of the manufacturers profile their channel partners using a huge variety of data ranging from birthday of the founder all the way down to the number of support people in place. The list is long and often has more than 50 questions. However, most of the data, once stored is never reviewed again. Even worse, the data is outdated within the next 6 to 12 months and almost nobody wants to maintain it – simply because it is not business-process relevant. There are very few pieces of information that are business relevant: These would include geographic coverage, along with special topics such as specific industry coverage or special customer type affinity, product coverage with details such as product training, experience and/or the ability to manage larger projects. Other than that it is important to know, on an ongoing basis, whether the sales strategy has changed or the financial situation has changed. This is already difficult enough to obtain other than through monitoring payment behavior.

Even the best PRM systems watch the channel from the manufacturer's viewpoint and require the manufacturer's channel sales people to maintain the data. But as we all know, this is not a scalable model and is even dangerous because it may limit the channel development due to limited internal resources not being able to cover a large channel. This method becomes damaging to channel development.

One alternative has been the development of partner portals where partners are asked to register and leave their footprint in order to get access to information. Information maintenance remains the biggest problem, and it still does not show current business activities, sales progress or any sales relevant information. Not all partners find the portal relevant and many do not use it.

3.2.3.4   Determining Profile Relevance

In order to define what is relevant for a partner profile, it is important to review what is relevant in the day-to-day business process. The function of a channel is a *leverage* model for sales. A channel does not develop or produce a product, does not brand or perform any major logistic function except stocking distributors. The main purpose of a channel is the remote self-motivated sales functionality. To leverage that system and to make the manufacturer successful by selling through the channel, the channel needs to be educated about the product. In turn, a product needs to be easy enough to sell through the channel with reasonable engagement requirements. Another important aspect, of course, is the target market reach of the channel. The channel needs to be able to cover the market the manufacturer wants to pursue. The channel partner that can reach the target market may be defined by geographic coverage, specific industry knowledge or specialization in certain types of customers. If a channel partner has access to the target market and is able to sell the manufacturer's solution, we already have a matching profile. Everything else may be interesting information but we have yet to see any other information to be business process relevant.

3.2.3.5 Additional Profiling

As mentioned earlier, it is also important to understand the financial situation of the channel partner in order to conduct a business relationship. This is information, which needs to be maintained by the manufacturer. Further details may be of interest but at this point, it is already based on very individual requirements from very individual sales people. A channel manager may or may not store the birthday of his key contact at the reseller organization with whom he is dealing.

Others may or may not want to maintain the number of support people the reseller had at the time he was authorized. And other people may have other very specific needs. But on a global scale, to market and sell to a channel, this information is not decision-relevant from a profile perspective.

But one kind of information would be very important to review when profiling a partner: the actual sales activity and sales results - as well as the constant change in personnel and focus. This is only possible if you have a robust channel and alliance management system in place.

3.2.3.6 Real-Time Profiling

We determined that real-time profiling is of utmost importance in managing a large-scale channel in an ever-changing business environment. To achieve real-time profiling a variety of elements need to work together.

We have two major aspects to real-time profiling: static profiling and dynamic profiling. Static profiling covers the classic aspects such as typical company data as well as territorial and product coverage. The dynamic profiling covers sales behavior, activity rate, relative sales closure rate, sales cycle information and sales initiatives.

3.2.3.7   Static Profiling

This aspect of the channel profile covers the channel partner's general information, which remains unchanged over time unless there are changes in personnel or business directions.

▶ **Self-Administration** – Every partner is not only a "reseller body" but a team of people, primarily in sales. It is key that all manufacturer-relevant people within that partner are covered by the system and can be maintained and administrated by the partner herself. The screenshot example shows a partner profile with a list of team members, maintained by the partner including a photo and elements from social networking. As team 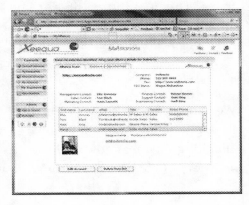 members change career, the confirmed alliances have an always up-to-date picture of their partners.

▶ **Territorial Coverage** – The territory a reseller can cover is dependent on its sales reach. Some partners have local offices or other sub-partners. In a manual PRM-like environment, these aspects are mostly ignored because it is too cumbersome to manage. If interest exists, such as specific customer-group focus, which may vary by outlet, the business partner needs to be able to express it and the system needs to incorporate it. For every opportunity that shows such a pattern the respective partner must be instantly identifiable. Modern system have the advantage to leverage latest technology such as Google Maps and position the partners on such a map instantaneously versus exporting data and creating a map based on data that are most of the time already out of date.

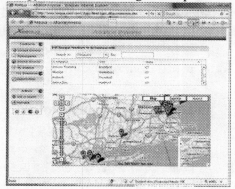

▶ **Product Coverage** - Channel partners will differ in product focus. Profiling needs to address this focus in order to provide the right information or to work on an adequate opportunity with such partners. Some may only work with parts of a manufacturer's product line and others may only work in a specific range of even the same product type. Some products may require authorization and training. Product coverage may change constantly as channel partners change their focus.

Changing product or market coverage aspects again requires self-administration by the channel partner in order to keep up to date. Adjusting the preferences of the channel partner's sales people relative to their sales leads is one way to keep his motivation to maintain the profile at the highest level. Over the past 2 years our experience shows that sales people are only interested in leads which are as close as possible to their profile. A match is part of the natural cycle.

3.2.3.8 Dynamic Profiling

Even more intriguing than the static profile is the dynamic profile development. By monitoring sales lead and opportunity follow-up sequences, the contact rate and closure rate, profiles change dynamically.

- **Follow-up Rate** – The follow-up rate shows the number of opportunities on which a partner is working relative to all opportunities available in that territory. The relativity takes out the argument of being in a geographically slow area. It shows engagement over time and allows decisions in terms of participation in campaigns, number of leads she may be able to take or even whether it makes sense to continue a partnership.

- **Closure Rate** – The closure rate shows the number of deals successfully closed relative to all deals that the partner is working. The closure rate determines the success profile of that given partner not only by closure but possibly even closure rate by product line, in order to determine the best kind of support that partner should receive.

- **Sales Cycle** – Sales cycle information provides a very detailed insight to the partner's success pattern and sales activity profile. Sales cycle information determines more than any other information, specific training and support needs during the partnership. Developing a partner means developing his profile.

As soon as it comes to sales lead distribution it is critical to understand who is active, engaged and very consistently going after new opportunities, and who is very project driven, busy for maybe 3 months until a project is completed and able to work on new opportunities.

Dynamic profiling is particularly important for channel-integrated marketing initiatives. We have discovered high friction with partners who want to do more than they are able to cover. On the other hand, partners may be powerful enough to handle nationwide projects but only for a fraction of the manufacturer's product line, while in specific regions other product sales show high results.

3.2.3.9 Self-Maintained Profiling

Again in today's PRM-like environment channel partners are managed like customers in a CRM system. The manufacturer keeps track of contacts, names, trainings, MDF funds and other data. The resources on the manufacturer-side often determine the size of the channel. In order to overcome this problem and use the channel as a true leverage model, profiling needs to be supported by the channel itself. Self-service is a very critical aspect to its maintainability and accurateness of its data. The single biggest problem how ever in PRM or Portal Systems is, that a partner dealing with many manufacturers won't be able to update all their manufacturers' systems unless all systems are somewhat networked together.

3.2.3.10 Covering Complexity

The complexity of a channel lies primarily in its diversity. Only a very diverse channel provides the leverage effect a manufacturer seeks. Channel partners are not a monolithic object with one key contact, but a living and changing structure of people: Inside sales, sales people on the street, sales managers and the owners or executives of those operations. In addition, these partners often have local offices, people in home offices in distant regions and other types of alliances, which may create interesting influence on the manufacturer's sales activities. Only 500 resellers may have a total of 1,000 locations. If they have 10 sales people on average (some may have only 1, others may have 100) per location, we are dealing with 10,000 sales people who have their own schedule, their own constantly changing priorities, and their own profiles. If the channel expands to a multi-national partner network, we may deal with 100,000 and more individuals on a dynamically changing basis. Profiling becomes virtually impossible if done by the manufacturer.

3.2.3.11 Channel Pattern

Each one of the participating partners and their sales people have their own interest in the engagement with the manufacturer. Some may just want information; others may want to constantly work jointly on deals. Again, here it is important to cover the relevant profiles. Somebody who is not interested in collaborating with the manufacturer but still purchases products through a distributor is important but is not worth profiling. In turn, somebody who is interested in doing deals with the manufacturer is relevant to profile.

Year after year, one of the things channel partners want most from their manufacturers is sales leads. This is where self-maintained profiles work best. The type of lead in which the partner is interested is the best profile to its sales and activity orientation. Whoever wants leads is required to profile himself in order to get the *right* leads. The vast majority of partners will maintain their profile because of the leads. The top partners, who are usually not interested in the manufacturer's sales leads, can easily be profiled by the manufacturer's channel sales crew and the rest of the channel can be captured for marketing activities but do not need to be profiled.

3.2.3.12 Reporting

Obviously it is key to monitor and measure any changes and drive the respective development. Here are some reports you should be able to create and it's respective business value:

3.2.3.13 Partner Distribution

Shows the number of partners (count and %)

a) by level (how many partners of each level do we have)

b) by Type (how many partners of each type do we have) and

c) by account type (how many partners of each account type do we have).

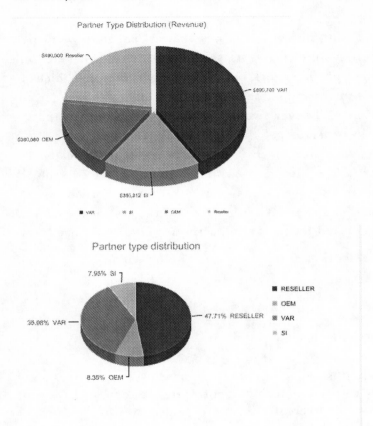

Business Value:

Partner Type Distribution: This report will show partner type distribution such as VARs, SIS, OEMs etc. It indicates in one chart the dominance in your channel both from a "numbers" point of view and from a "revenue amount" point of view. Often seen is a huge number of some group but producing just a very small portion of the revenue stream.

Top 10 Territories:

Shows the Top 10 territories by revenue and the rest in one piece of the pie

Top 10 territories by revenue

$129,090 FL
$120,005 OTHER
$32,000 UT
$129,900 MA
$246,000 TX
$90,000 MI
$50,000 NC
$80,000 SC
$120,000 NY

FL
MA
MI
NC
NY
SC
TX
UT
OTHER

TOP TEN Partners (Revenue in USD)

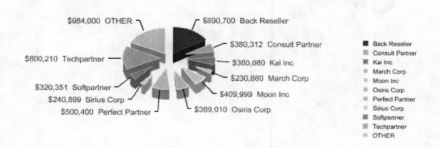

$984,000 OTHER
$890,700 Back Reseller
$380,312 Consult Partner
$800,210 Techpartner
$380,080 Kai Inc
$320,351 Softpartner
$230,880 March Corp
$240,899 Sirius Corp
$409,999 Moon Inc
$500,400 Perfect Partner
$389,010 Osiris Corp

Back Reseller
Consult Partner
Kai Inc
March Corp
Moon Inc
Osiris Corp
Perfect Partner
Sirius Corp
Softpartner
Techpartner
OTHER

Business Value:

Provides manufacturers with instant visibility into the performance of their 10 top territories (by percentage/by revenue). It provides an interesting view how strong the top 10 territories influence the business and what potential can be uncovered in other territories. This report should be used in conjunction with the report "Partner Coverage by Type" (#14) to identify the possibility of growth for traditionally strong territories.

Partner Coverage By Enablement

Shows the number of active (enabled) partners in each region. Filter by functional enablement. "All" meaning partners who are enabled for all functions.

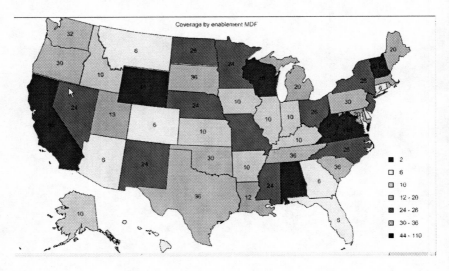

3.2.3.14   Thought Leadership

Developing channel partner profiling systems and finally finding ways to maintain them require a very detailed analysis of what is really relevant and what keeps the relevant information up to date. The guiding thoughts have been:

- What is important to a channel sales manager in order to develop his business partners and monitor his entire channel?

- What decisions are being made during the life time of a partner relationship that lead to improved performance other than managing ad hoc activities?

- How can we be sure that the information is constantly maintained not only for a few top partners, but also across the entire channel organization?

- What would be the most important set of information to ensure the highest possible influence in the sales process?

The result was not to automate partner forms on partner portals but generate a dynamically changing profiling pattern.

Channel Excellence Methodology suggests that you create a partner profile for each market segment you try to address and the respective attributes you expect from the channel partners. In addition, you define the dynamic parameters that give you an indication of development and progress and have your channel representatives be responsible for developing the respective partners. With a supporting system in place, even large channels can be developed as long as the data can be transformed in respective reports.

3.2.4. Channel Creation.

This section discusses how to actually create a channel.

> Synopsis: Most of the time channel sales just happens when a product or service becomes successful and has created demand. At some point a company needs to create an "official" channel. This step determines the way and the success of the channel like no other event. Everything after that point will be a result of that official channel architecture.

As long as VARs, catalyst, SIs or other channel organizations demand cooperation because their customers want the manufacturer's products, pretty much every mistake in the interaction can be somewhat forgiven because of the nature of the request. But if a company officially declares that a channel will be developed, partners get acquired and companies are encouraged to collaborate – all of a sudden every mistake counts ten times the weight. Therefore, I highly suggest that companies take their time and be very careful with the rollout of a channel strategy. Too many companies failed in their first few attempts to create a channel and had a very hard time coming back to try again. The actual creation of a channel is an architectural event: more time and high-level energy goes into the planning process than in the building process. Once building starts, the plan needs to be rock solid. As the subtitle of the book says: "<u>Architecting,</u> Managing and Accelerating Indirect Business" the *architecting* is the first step and a cornerstone in the whole channel business.

Once the target market is understood and the channel sizing (see previous chapters) is completed, you and the potential partners should have a good understanding of how many partners in what kind or territories are needed over time. In architectural speak: You should know how many rooms you need, how big they need to be and therefore how big the house should be. As a second major step you will need to create a partner profile sufficient to capture the desired market and able to successfully win and service the customers. Again in architect's language: Now we decide what kind of rooms we need in our house and what kind of purpose they serve.

Now comes the most difficult part for both channel architects and architects building homes: Defining how the flow should be. How we reach the rooms, how far should it be from kitchen to dining room, to family room, to the back yard. How we will reach the rooms when we come from the garage or the entry, how we bring our clothes to the laundry, how it feels when guests enter the home and how the kids can have fun in one section while parents may work in either the same or in an opposite area. This part of architecting a home actually defines an excellent architecture from a convoluted cheap home plan. It is the same with our channel architecture.

Architecting a channel means architecting the flow of all the business processes between partners and manufacturers. Regardless of whether there are distributors in between. This has nothing to do with creating a price list or a loyalty program. It has nothing to do with dividing channel partners into gold, silver or bronze categories. It has nothing to do with the discount structure. The channel architecture is the definition of the business process interaction with the channel. It describes how leads are handed over from the manufacturer to the partner, how a partner can get technical support from the manufacturer, how orders are processed, how returns are handled, how information is distributed and how a partner can interact with all kinds of departments within the manufacturer's corporate structure.

The channel architecture is the manufacturer's internal workflow for each aspect of the manufacturer/partner relationship. If this is well thought out and *very* easy for a partner, it is so much more likely to be a successful partnership. To create a successful channel a manufacturer needs to adopt the best practices that are used in the respective industry and partner's need to confirm the ease of interaction. Most of the following chapters describe best practices in the interaction between partners and manufacturers.

3.2.5.   Building a SaaS Channel

This section discusses differences in SaaS versus traditional IT channels and what is needed to build a successful SaaS channel.

> **Synopsis:** Channel recruitment is easier than one may think. As soon as a clear channel strategy is in place and the necessary basic resources are available channel recruiting can begin. The most important part is to define what kind of partners is needed in which territories to address what market needs. A self-selection process on the channel-side will support this engagement more than the coolest recruitment program.

After spending some 3 years with manufacturers, consultants and users in the SaaS industry my view about a SaaS channel has matured quite a bit. Here is the 30,000-foot viewpoint and why channels in the SaaS industry are fundamentally different from their counterparts in the traditional IT world

- In SaaS, there are no products on which a reseller has a title. There is no inventory or logistics, no contractual reselling activity, no repair service and no physical goods to install or connect.

- The main focus in the SaaS world is on business process alignment, optimizing the use of the information, solution deployment, application support and integration in existing systems

- While products have been sold and the user has been on her own from then on – SaaS solutions are sold in an ongoing services manner. Analogous to the application provider model – services should be provided in a very similar recurring model, the "Recurring Services Model".

- As SaaS manufacturers host the application, they become effectively the IT organization for their customers. Hence, tech support is a manufacturer internal activity. That fact will result in a very different employee structure and allow lower cost services.

- With an estimated 10 million companies using SaaS worldwide in the next 5-10 years, the SaaS industry will provide business opportunities for approximately 200,000 partner companies.

- Because of the very different structure we decided to give this new channel a new name – CATALYSTS

- Catalysts are companies or even some individuals who understand the various business needs in terms of organizational improvements in areas such as sales, marketing, HR, operations, logistics, etc. and also understand the advantages of SaaS-based applications.

- Catalysts will help small, medium and larger firms to transform their cumbersome "Information Technology" into "Information Management" by outsourcing the technology and applications and accelerate the use of the information itself.

3.2.5.1 Top Ten Aspects for Developing a Successful Catalyst Channel

The SaaS industry is new. The way SaaS catalysts do their business is new, and so is the partner engagement for manufacturers in this new world. Creating a successful catalyst channel is of essence if a manufacturer wants to compete on a global basis.

Partnership Spirit – The most important aspect of a successful partnership is that the spirit of collaborating is based on a joint engagement for a win-win situation. If channels are seen as an external sales force that has to take care on its business while the manufacturer takes care of her business – allowing competition between partners, the problem starts right there. The most successful channels – across industries – are the ones where channel conflict is alleviated and all the energy is focused on jointly winning more customers and gaining more market share.

Target Market – There may be customers, market segments or geographies where a manufacturer wants to or needs to operate directly. As long as everybody knows and everybody sticks to the rules, this would be perfectly fine. Let your catalyst partners know what you are doing and you will develop trust.

If there is a breach of trust – there is another manufacturer. It is always helpful to select partners for specific target markets where you as a manufacturer are not likely to succeed by going direct or have no resources to cover.

Compensation – Compensating the partners for finding new customers is more difficult in the SaaS industry than in the traditional IT industry. Setting expectations and having clear concepts is of the essence. Many SaaS companies still struggle to adequately compensate their internal sales teams, let alone have a compensation plan for partners. Therefore, I have made some suggestions:

▶ **Referral Fee** – Paying a 15% referral fee for the first year's recurring revenue payable in the cycles the customer has to pay should be adequate to motivate a catalyst to start actively promoting the solution and compensate him for his sales engagement. The fee should be similar but less than your internal cost of sales. If you can sell direct at less cost – sell direct as long as you can.

▶ **Renewal Fee** – As contract renewals are not a given but less difficult than identifying a new customer, I suggest an 8% renewal compensation if the catalyst is continuing to serve the customer and the customer does not require the manufacturer to replace the catalyst.

▶ **Coop Marketing Funds** – Provide an additional 3% coop-marketing fund where you help catalysts create local events or activities that help identify new customers. The 3% should be matched by the same amount from the catalyst in order to ensure that the money is spent wisely. The 3% is based on the revenue that the catalyst made with you as a manufacturer.

This model may not work with established consulting firms or VARs but if this is not attractive to them – they will not be a fit anyway.

Training – Do not make the mistakes of the "old world" and charge your partner for training. Provide at least quarterly web casts and try to train your catalyst team as well as you possibly can. Catalysts will assemble best of breed solutions for their customers, and they will suggest what they know best. Focus training on the business process and usability-side as the catalysts will focus on that with their customers.

Partner Programs – Partner programs are an essential component in a partner strategy in general and with catalysts in particular. Rewarding partners for engagement is a natural behavior and should be applied to catalyst partners as it would to any other partner. A good practice could be rewards based on number of deployments. This would reflect the ability to execute, ability to build repeating processes and ability to help grow market share. This blended with a second component: Customer Satisfaction gives the reward a deep meaning and can help others to grow in exactly the direction we all have to grow: With more satisfied customers.

Services Demarcation – It is highly suggested that manufacturers and partners have a very clear understanding of who provides which services and where those services interface. At least in emerging companies, the manufacturer fears more to dissatisfy a customer than to lose a partner. In order to reduce this as a potential conflict, it would be very important to draw a Service Map that shows the service flow and the interfaces between the parties. Let me provide an example:

► **Deployment** – The manufacturer releases the application to the customer, provides an user ID and password and confirms the availability of the service. The catalyst then does any configuration of the system. The catalyst is educated enough to fully understand the application in the present release.

► **Integration** – The manufacturer helps with integration up to the interface level and data definition. The catalyst acts as a project lead between manufacturers and customer. Any technical work in integrating two SaaS manufacturers would be done by the manufacturers, unless the catalyst acquired special skills. The catalyst would provide help to the customer to move data back and forth.

► **Training** – The catalyst would provide all trainings to the customer. If the manufacturer prefers to handle the trainings then that would simply be the rule, but it should be clear and not random.

► **Support** – The catalyst is the first line of support. The catalyst should be equipped enough to verify whether a system is down, a bug is identified or to identify an issue as a usage issue.

► **Additional Services** – The manufacturer should remain having a close relationship to the customer and offer him additional features or functionality.

► **Joint service log** – It would be a good practice for manufacturers and partners to share their experience and activities with their joint customers in order to ensure that all parties know what is going on. If manufacturer and partner worry about competing with each other that would obviously not work out.

Joint Marketing & Sales - Once a relationship and, more importantly, trust is established with a catalyst, joint selling and marketing will become very important. Providing sales leads to the catalyst partner can offload the manufacturer's sales organization and leverage the partner while the partner can grow based on those leads. On the other hand, as the number of catalysts grow into the thousands, it will be important to understand on what kind of deals which partner is working so a central deal registration may become important. Supporting the partners with marketing funds is key in the joint engagement for more market share.

Once you go international with your product, partnerships will add better reach in sales and provide better services for your overseas customers.

Channel Conflict – As stated in the first paragraph, channel conflict is the biggest obstacle in any channel strategy in any industry. Companies in all industries loose more money and efficiency in channel conflict issues than any other corporate issue and with any other corporate investment including research and development and marketing. If a direct sales team believes in competition, I suggest removing all structures and letting the internal sales people freely compete against each other.

Do not "try" indirect business models. Once a partner community is burned with mistakes, it is very hard and costly to recover. Do it right in the first place.

Leadership – A channel strategy, like any other go to market strategy, needs to be endorsed by the CEO of a company. If the leadership team is not behind the channel strategy, I suggest to any catalyst not to engage unless the strategy is clear and public. As part of the strategy put a C-level member in charge of partner management who can ensure the prevention of any channel conflicts.

3.2.6.   Partner Recruiting

This section discusses best practices in recruiting new channel partners based on the required size a channel needs to be. It also discusses channel strategy and corporate objectives as well as resource requirements.

> **Synopsis**: Partner recruitment is easier than one may think. As soon as a clear channel strategy is in place and the necessary basic resources are available channel recruiting can begin. Once the profile of the ideal partner is established and the territories are defined, it doesn't take much to recruit partners. Announcing partner programs in the trade press typically creates the first buzz – and it will spread quickly after the first success stories.

Resellers, VARs, agents, and distributors are companies that have developed their own profile in terms of addressable market, core competencies, and products they are interested in reselling or servicing. If your channel program resonates with their profile you should engage them.

Recruiting business partners is rather similar to recruiting employees: It is highly recommended that whoever is recruiting new people has a clear profile and needs analysis, defines what type of business needs to be developed and identifies people who match the profile.

Setting up a recruitment system that is not thoughtful or thorough can be costly and even dangerous to your business. I have seen companies who simply wanted resellers to do the sales job they could not do themselves. Other examples I came across were companies who actually hired other firms to search for channel partners and run their channel. Even so there are cases where this worked very well. Of course, there is an equal risk that it may fail simply because the channel recruiting firm does not have the right setup to perform the job.

There are many cases where companies simply added resellers to enlarge their list. The partners were even introduced to customers, but with no upfront education. In almost all cases this method struck back like a boomerang when the competition built a well-defined channel strategy and basically just "harvested" that existing channel by offering a well thought out channel program, sold into the partners accounts and intelligently competed on the other manufacturer's turf.

Partner recruiting should not start before all the strategic questions are answered, programs are in place, marketing is fired up and all other aspects from logistics, margin/fee structure, training and support etc. are well formulated and in place.

Starting the recruiting process from this point in time is not really that difficult. The optimal way is to select a very small but important group of partners covering the respective target market and working with them on the entire channel program before a broader recruiting process begins. These partners not only help verify the channel strategy but also help spread the word. Like in any other business, opinion leaders will be a great draw for other partners to follow. One of the most successful ways to recruit partners is in combination with a lead distribution program. Providing sales leads to partners demonstrates a few important things: a) there is demand hence the leads are there, b) the manufacturer is willing to share opportunities with partners and not take them direct, and c) with new leads there is an instant way of entering the market with a new product or brand. Also, this can be easily used for a press release that also demonstrates publicly that this manufacturer is entering the channel.

Another good practice is to start a road show, introducing the company in person to the new potential channel partners. As we said earlier, partners should be treated like employees and there are not many cases where people get hired without ever seeing anybody from the company. The partner relationship is very much also a personal business relationship that is supposed to hold over many years. If the cost for that interaction is too high, maybe it is too early to engage with partners. The event itself does not need to be a big show. It needs to be informative and personal. Whenever I held tours, I did "On a beer events," simply let people know in which city I would be and invited them for a beer in a local pub. It was a quick introduction, some talk about the company and the product and the rest was small talk. It was the best way to get to know each other and to get a sense of whether you wanted to do business together. The budget was really just a few hundred dollars per event.

In particular by leveraging the Internet partner recruiting was never so easy. Ziff Davis supports manufacturers by leveraging the publishers contact list and advertises directly to their readership. Computer Reseller News has similar mechanisms and allows mailing campaigns jointly with the manufacturers. The cost for those campaigns is moderate.

Another, newer resource is the Xeequa partner finder, a public directory of thousands of high tech VARs, resellers, catalysts and distributors around the world. End of 2007 there were over 30,000 VARs, resellers and system integrators listed. The directory is publicly available at no cost.

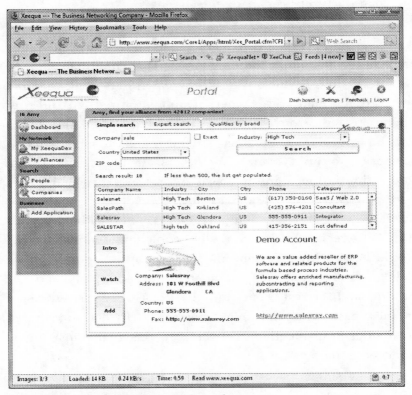

Screenshot Xeequa Partner Search

Partner Recruiting Checklist

Check the following bullets and see if you are ready to engage with a channel. Even so this book may help you with all the foundation and provide you with the fundamentals you may want to consider hiring a consulting firm that helps you implement a channel and do it right from the first time.

1) Did you completely solve a potential channel conflict? Do you have rules in place that makes it very clear for each deal whether and how it is sold?

2) Is your PRODUCT and your BACKOFFICE channel ready? Do you have the procedures, contracts, support and financial mechanism in place to roll out a channel?

3) Do you know what markets that channel shall serve and what the profile of those partners is? Do you know how many partners you would need to lead the market?

4) Is your partner program financially and operationally compelling enough to attract new partners?

5) Did you test your strategy, program and initiative with a few partners and received a positive feedback?

Always keep in mind that most partners have seen hundreds of manufacturers come and go. Every year thousands of companies get funding and start a new business with products so compelling that channel partners should bag to resell their partners. 12 to 24 month later those companies "expired". So don't expect great excitement about your offering but remember that channel partners ONLY get excited if they made their customers successful – not over a new technology.

Channel Excellence Methodology suggests that after sizing the channel, manufacturers who want to recruit partners need to conduct a thorough partner profile analysis (see previous chapters) and create a channel eco-system that attracts the right partners. Rather than having a loose registration process, interested partners should register in a system that captures the respective data points so that the partner analysis and selection process can occur almost instantaneously. In any event, it is important to establish a good personal relationship between partner and company – both teams should meet at least once.

3.2.7.   Channel Conflicts

This section discusses the most difficult aspect of channel creation – overcoming the channel conflict issue and building a powerful and highly engaged indirect sales force that is able to compete with virtually any competitor.

> **Synopsis**: Channel conflicts exist in most companies, yet it is the most distracting force and the least understood problem. In order to successfully compete in the market, it is of outmost importance that the competing forces within the partnership work in a zero friction environment.

The two wildest stories I heard about channel conflicts came from companies who were very adamant about their successful channel engagement. One was relatively young software company. The VP of sales told me: "If the partners cannot compete with my team – they are not worth it; I want better sales people than my own." That manager surely had trouble. He didn't even believe in his own team and wanted external sales people who were even better. His big thing was competition anywhere and under any circumstance. He actually created competition in order to just have it. Neither his own team nor his channel team was ever successful. Competitors even with weaker products and less funding outperformed that company within two years after they burned through all the funding.

The other story happened at a hardware manufacturer who request to put "Lost to partners" as a sales status feedback in the opportunity report. This company, even though they tried hard to grow a channel, could not overcome the fact that their own sales people should "win" if there is any competition – even a partner.

Hundreds of those stories are around the world, driven by a fatal ego to compete for competition sake not to win. In both the above cases and most other situations the term "competition" seemed to be completely misunderstood.

The only competition for a manufacturer should be the OTHER manufacturer but not their channel or any other alliance partner.

After all these years, I have come to see the direct/indirect question as an exclusivity question. Today I would rather run a 100% direct sales force then a 50/50 or any other mix. As I stated in the introduction where I explored differences between Compaq, Novell, Microsoft, Dell and their respective competitors the most successful sales organizations are the ones who exclusively focus on one sales strategy. Whether it is Dell's direct sales model or Microsoft's indirect sales model, both are extremely successful while the rest who mix models and change them every other year loose way too much energy. And as a partner I obviously would rather work with a clean indirect only company than with a company who has a direct sales force that will one day compete with me – regardless how "cool" the product appears to be.

The overall competition in a near saturated market is way too busy to allow for any game in the sales mix. At the same time cost of sales is one of the single biggest line items in every companies P+L; adjusting the model can be deadly. That said, the response I hear again and again is: "And that is exactly the reason why I can't risk going exclusively indirect. If the channel doesn't work out I may lose my company."

The question then becomes, "How to prevent channel conflict as one of the most costly friction points in a sales organization?" One answer is almost automatically offered when it comes to international sales. Most companies cannot afford an international direct sales force and channels are created based on demand, lack of direct presence and the presence of highly organized resellers, consultants and distributors. If that does not work out, then the international business is in jeopardy and the company is at great risk of losing the game against the competition.

Since we know the international channel will work out, why not establish a domestic US channel? It is not so much a risk as it is the direct sales leaders who simply do not want to lose their jobs. And so the real conflict is not a channel conflict but an internal management issue as a company needs to transform itself from direct to indirect.

3.3. Methodologies for Partner Marketing

How to setup effective Partner Marketing, compete in the field and grow market share

3.4.1 Partner Marketing

3.4.2 Channel Programs

3.4.3 Demand Creation

3.4.4 Collaborative Marketing (MDF & Coop)

3.3.1. Partner Marketing

This section discusses marketing in the context of channel marketing, what the channel has to do with branding, awareness and demand generation. Exploring who needs to contribute to marketing and in what way.

Synopsis: Marketing is one of the key strategic initiatives around channel sales, yet it is very often completely underestimated and misinterpreted when developing channel marketing initiatives. At this point we do not need to discuss the value of marketing but the structure of marketing to certain target groups.

Partner Marketing is a wholly own discipline to market a company and its products and services into a channel – it is neither to sell through the channel nor to sell to the channel. Like the energy to attract employees, partner marketing shall attract partners and keep them attracted.

Partner or Channel marketing is a stand-alone discipline, like product marketing and corporate marketing. While product marketing helps to market a product and delivers all the necessary ingredients, channel marketing helps to market into a channel and delivers all the necessary ingredients to attract a channel, motivate a channel and grow a channel by helping the channel market itself. Channel marketing is NOT the marketing through the channel to the end customer – this is corporate marketing, whether it helps branding or selling.

One of the key marketing initiatives (not channel marketing) is to create brand awareness and generate demand. At the end both goes hand in hand. Good marketing always associates demand generation with brand awareness.

It is important to share those initiatives with the partners and have a mechanism in place to let partners participate in those campaigns and leverage them for their own markets.

It is a very good practice to clearly describe what channel marketing is to provide and how the company's corporate and product marketing interacts with the channel. Too often every marketing interaction with the partner is pushed into "Partner Marketing" and partners hear from a campaign by reading blogs, news or other media. Partners can add an enormous lever to any marketing campaign if they are aware right from the creation on. It is not necessary but a good idea to check the partners' opinion as well. But at least partners should know what is coming. Imagine this:

Company A has 1,000 partners and is creating a campaign, blasting it to their customer base of 5,000 and offering a discount for the next 2 weeks. Partners hear about it and may or may not cram it into their own customer base leaving them with maybe just 1 week.

Company B has only 500 partners and limited marketing funds but makes the campaign available to their partners who have another 50,000 customers. Before a year is out, Company B will be taking over Company A, just by leveraging every partner they have.

Please note: This is not a partner marketing responsibility. This is a corporate marketing task. Partner marketing's job is to attract partners and keep them attracted.

So, "What exactly is partner marketing doing?" you may ask. First and foremost, it is recruiting: running campaigns to attract new partners, communicating the values of a partnership, explaining the programs and the support initiatives, showing the education program, demonstrating the joint selling mechanism and the interaction with the manufacturer's team.

I was consulting a large security company and reviewing their "partner marketing activities." Every piece that company produced read like a legal document. Every initiative was explained very well, but was very dry. The whole collaboration sounded like a contract with the devil. As long as the patented technology was in high demand, partners went through the painful process but as alternatives appeared in the market, partners were running as fast as they came. Theoretically, it would be easy to rewrite the material and make it fun and attractive, but after years of practicing the old way, the whole company culture was infiltrated by the dry and boring procedures. The company is still today struggling with re-vamping their channels.

So Channel Marketing is more than just recruiting; it is the ongoing communication between company and the partners' teams. That said, the point is the team not "the partner." Like everything else in marketing a robust and most current database is of the essence. In today's connected world it is expected that certain information is provided to specific people, rather than overwhelming the whole team with everything. A CRN study from 2005 showed that an individual within an average reseller organization is receiving 80 emails a week from their various manufacturers. There is just not enough time to read it all – in many cases there is not even enough time to prioritize them. Also here the messages need to be attractive and make sense for the target group.

Typical channel marketing campaigns are channel specific promotions, industry alerts, competitive information updates, training opportunities, performance rankings and other channel specific activities, events or rewards.

Also here, reporting is very critical to understand the success of the program and its development. The example below shows a development of partners by type over time.

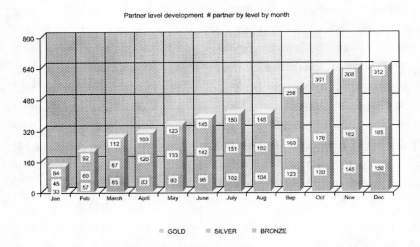

Partner level development # partner by level by month

Clearly those activities need a budget and need to be planned. And as channel marketing activities are not product sales initiatives or other marketing campaigns, channel marketing is often created as a percentage of last quarters revenue rather than a forward looking investment. Only in the first year a channel marketing budget should be defined and allow the channel team to build or overhaul their channel.

Channel Excellence Methodology suggests a clear separation from end user marketing and any kind of product or brand promotions on one side and the channel creation and development initiatives on the other side. Channel marketing is to recruit and then motivate and further develop the partnership.

3.3.2.　　Channel Programs

This section discusses what kind of channel programs help develop the channel, help the channel to drive more business and help the company to generate more successes. It also discusses partner programs from both sides, the partner and the manufacturer, and explores how well designed programs help change behaviors without unwanted manipulation. Finally, it explores some successful partner programs, discussing how modern methodologies and new technologies affect partner programs and demonstrating how loyalty programs have lesser importance than programs that add value to the partners.

> **Synopsis**: Check with your top, mid and bottom tier partners before you roll out a new program. Make sure that there is something in it for the partners such as tech support, sales support, marketing support, operations support, new business, profits, or competitive advantage. Build a program with measurable goals and explain why you are doing the program. Make the program available to a wide audience and select the partners you actually work with in that program. To manage the program, use a system that helps you to keep track of the participants of each program. Do not try loyalty programs – "Ain't gonna work."

Let me start with another anecdote: We were about to roll out a brand new partner program for one of our clients and interviewed a handful of partners to get their opinion. One of the partners started: "Before you tell me anything about this new program: Who is behind this program from your executive team?" My answer: "Everybody, even the CEO" He responded, "OK then I'll pull in my team. Sorry for asking, but I've just seen too many programs that sounded great, but for whatever reason were all of a sudden discontinued. I do not want to put my team behind ideas you guys want to 'try out'. We don't have the patience anymore to be quite frank."

The top 10 elements you should check when you develop a program before you even introduce it internally:

1. Program name

2. What is the goal of the program?

3. Which of your partners should participate?

4. When shall the program start and how long shall it run?

5. What do you expect the partner's teams (typically sales people) to actually do when they participate?

6. What is the motive for the partner to participate?

7. What is the motive for your internal team to support it?

8. What do you consider success?

9. How do you measure success?

10. Do think this program is fun to do?

Be rather precise with the goal. "Incremental Revenue" should not be the answer to the "Goal of the program" because this is the reason you have a channel ;-). However, it may be bringing the revenue from X to Y for a particular product, or grow revenue by x% above market growth. In any case, it is not very intriguing for the channel partners to bring *your* revenue up by x%. But you can achieve your goal by asking the partners to increase *their* revenue for a certain product by x%. First, this is much easier to do from the partner's perspective, and secondly, the results would be more rewarding for the partners.

The typical partner classifications - "Gold, Silver, Bronze" - are partner segmentation programs. Those are important to segment your channel and allow you to apply certain pricing models or marketing engagements. However, I do not consider those really "Partner Programs." See partner segmentation under the chapter "Methodologies for Channel Operation."

Here are two examples of partner programs. One that worked very well and one that did not work at all:

- Indiana Jones Program

- The XYZ Official Partner Program

Indiana Jones Program

Of course it was many years ago and could be the "DaVinci" Program" today. The whole program wrapped around the Indiana Jones theme, starting with the promotional material, the rewards, the goals and all the little things like price lists and the final awards meeting.

The idea promoted new hard disk systems against a variety of existing manufacturers. The systems did not have any major technical advantages but did have a very good-looking enclosure. We needed to introduce this new product from an unknown manufacturer against major competition.

The goal for the partner: The winner would receive a treasure box including a flight to a foreign island, cash, a watch and other desirable items.

What was the goal of the program?

We needed to successfully compete and win market share. Furthermore, we wanted to engage twice as many partners in selling the product as we had at the beginning of the promotion and we wanted to win 10 strategic, named accounts. So the goal was rather complex:

- 5% more market share (almost 30% more revenue back)

- Doubling of partner mindshare (from 250 to 500 active partners)

- Increase of strategic end customers (10 from a list of 100)

Which kind of partners did we want to participate?

We wanted to engage all our partners but also partners from our competitors. We needed to motivate new partners who were not so much into the hardware products but had access to large account through their systems expertise. This was our strategic initiative to access the large accounts. We did not have too much time to slice and dice and qualify the possible partners: Our approach was the more the better. We developed a list of about 1,800 resellers who sort of matched the profile.

When did the program start and how long did it run?

The program started September 1 and last for 4 months until Christmas.

What did we expect the partners' teams (typically sales people) to actually do when they participated?

We wanted our partners to select one of the three goals they thought might fit their profile best and assign 3 people internally to support the respective groups.

Group 1 was focused with our existing partners to grow market share by doubling their current revenue specific to the hard disk systems. We wanted the partners to go back to their installed base and offer the new solution, invite these customers to their stores for an in-store presentation and support our end-user road show.

Group 2 was asked to consider our new system to introduce to their customers and engage in a partnership with us, something they did not do before. Our partner team was charged with recruiting partners and having them sell at least one system by year-end. By building 250 partnerships, we would increase by at least 250 additional systems.

Group 3 supported a small team of partners who would actually engage their large accounts and asked to make a presentation jointly with us.

What was the motive for the partners to participate?

The motive was, depending on the group:

> ➤ more revenue relative to what they earn today and our support to help execute,

> ➤ a new manufacturer who was totally behind the channel, and

> ➤ a good chance for some of the partners to sell the new system and improve their relationship with their large accounts.

What was the motive for our internal team to support it?

The group who achieved the goal would join the winners on a foreign Indiana Jones Island, and it was a lot of fun to execute the program.

What did we consider success?

If one of the 3 goals had been achieved we would have considered the campaign a great success.

How did we measure success?

$1 million in incremental revenue, 250 partners that sell the product and 10 corporate accounts who purchased one of the systems.

Did we think this program was fun to do?

YES! It was the most fun program we ever did.

All participants received a map to the hidden treasure. The paths showed key milestones to reach the hidden treasure. The milestones were not cities or landmarks but sales steps. Once in a while we would send Indiana Jones video tapes, little gadgets, a status overview of how the teams were doing and Indiana Jones Island brochures where the winner would go to reap her reward.

In the end, we had close to 1,000 partners selling the systems, 38 large customers who bought one or more products and $3 million in incremental revenue. Furthermore, we received an award for the most successful hard disk subsystem in the market.

The "XYZ Official Partner Program"

Here is an example of a program that needed substantial overhaul:

The program was primarily designed to sign up partners. The goal was to get better-qualified partners. The manufacturer sent out a renewed partner contract of about 18 pages of legal document. The cover letter explained that company XYZ intends to improve the partner quality and will keep an elite set of partners. Any partner who wanted to participate needed to sign the contract.

Many partners did not sign up. In particular, the top partners found it boring and only the partners who were dependent on that manufacturer signed up. Motivation was pretty much down. The manufacturer continued to serve all the partners they had, with or without contract. The program was not continued and everything was back to the way it was before – neither better nor worse.

Clearly, this was a learning experience however the learning did not happen. Now after 5 years the channel program is still unchanged. A substantial overhaul was recommended by the companies channel team but the executives are so "serious" that nothing but legally reviewed papers would leave the post out. Between 2000 and early 2007 6 channel managers were hired and fired. In that case the problem is clearly not the channel marketing team but the company culture. Every program has go through the legal department for whatever reason, the CFO checks channel marketing initiatives and feels this is all a waste of time and money. At the same time the CEO is in particular proud on his direct sales team.

In any case, there is a lot of middle ground between the two programs mentioned. Programs may need some legal eyes to double check whether everything in the offer is legally correct. However the partner should not require a lawyer to sign up. It may not be a multi-team engagement but fun should be an integral part of a program.

A partner program needs to provide some benefit for the partner. It may be as illustrated in the previous example, sales support from your side. It may be technical support where you invest in your channel. If you can provide some competitive advantage, you have the ear of your partners guaranteed. Like you, your partner competes in the market. If you can help your partner to compete against your competition or others, you can provide a huge benefit to your partners. You may help compete not only by providing aggressive pricing (Sure, that is the easiest way to do it.), but you may provide very focused marketing support instead to drive end customer attention to your partner. In particular if your partner competes with another partner of yours, you do not necessarily give the engaged partner simply a better price, give him a reward for his engagement. Market visibility is a huge motive for partners to engage.

In particular, with larger channels, it is very important to keep track of which partner is actually engaging in a given program. Make the program in such a way that the initial engagement requires the partner not only join the program, but have her assign a person who will drive the program within the channel partner. Another form of commitment is asking her to name five accounts of hers she wants to engage. Here you will see very quickly who is really engaged and who is not. Have the partners and their assigned people register in your system and help your own channel representatives keep track of who signed up for which campaign. Then execute with the partners who have signed up for those campaigns. As long as participation is a loose group, it is next to impossible to track results and measure success.

A program management system as part of a PRM or IRP system is the technical backbone to program management. Those systems need to support the above components such as participation, program name and definition, life cycle and reporting. If it is integrated into other components of the system the program success will be visible in the partner profiles and, over time, will give a good indication of your partner engagement and active participation.

Channel Excellence Methodology suggests always having very clearly measurable goals and a very good motive for partners to participate. Like always check it with a few key partners first before you launch it. Also – don't make it a disaster if the program fails, instead support a try and learn culture WITH you partners.

3.3.3.   Demand Creation

This section discusses why channel partners really cannot and should not create demand.

> **Synopsis**: Demand is a behavior from a market that is typically created by a brand or new technology or feature. The brand or IP owner is typically the creator of that demand. In order to capture that opportunity there is an important function of fulfillment. Fulfillment in any way or shape is typically provided by either the companies' logistics or service operation or through partners. Hoping partners can CREATE demand is a widely seen misperception.

Often times, manufacturers expect from their channel partners that they engage in demand generation, at least lead generation. There is often a big disappointment on the manufacturer side and frustration on the partner site.

Even if a reseller of any kind has a very big budget—he is most likely not able to CREATE DEMAND. He cannot attract a buyer or decision maker with its reseller brand; he is not able to represent the position of the product creator and is clearly never able to compete with other brands from within its reseller position. An indirect channel is the extension of the manufacturer's sales force. It is the extension in terms of selling people power into industries, markets, geographies or similar aspects. An indirect channel may be a service extension with the same aspects, but is not an extension of the manufacturers marketing organization – simply because it is a legally independent organization.

Partners shall and will be able to fulfill demand, as well as introduce the new product or service to his installed base. But if there is no demand, the introduction does not create demand. This may sound very much like "nickel and diming" but is of great importance to understand the partners role in marketing and to alleviate any frustration or disappointments.

Let us start with marketing. We all can agree that demand generation needs to be very closely associated with brand awareness in order to ensure that the newly created demand is driven home to the brand. Now a channel partner may have a brand, but this is different than the manufacturer brand. A good partner, carrying several manufacturer brands is at best associated with the collection of brands or with its own brand based on its specific identity – almost never identical with the manufacturer's own unique brand. This makes demand generation for a partner hard in the first place.

Partners are happy to identify themselves with the manufacturer's brand, if there is any, but that does not generate demand. If the partner would use the manufacturer's brand and create demand the manufacturer is not able to create in the first place, the question will come up why this is the case? Budget? If the manufacturer does not have the budget, the partner needs to have it. The only budget resource for the partner is the margin after it initially sells enough products to generate the extra margin to start brand and demand creation. This is not likely to happen, so the only other source would be what the partner invests. This investment would have been created with margin he earned from other products, which we know is not big enough either. So channel partners are financially not able to create demand for a manufacturer that is not able to create the demand itself.

Now a manufacturer may think, there is not much to create – simply talk to your existing customers...

Channel Excellence Methodology suggests that you help your partners to address their local installed base but do not expect the channel partners to create demand. Instead you, the manufacturer creates the demand, using your brand and the fact that you are the creator of the product that is recommended through the channel.

3.3.4.   Collaborative Marketing (MDF & Coop)

This section discusses how to leverage funds with partners marketing power and budgets.

> **Synopsis**: Doubling your marketing budget with the partners budget and leverage each other to mutual business success.

In 2005 Cisco reported more than $3Million in unclaimed coop marketing funds. Partners who were eligible for marketing funds simply did not take advantage of them a lost opportunity for both: manufacturer and partner. As the name says; Coop Funds stands for cooperative marketing funds. Cooperative, because both partners leverage each other. The manufacturer puts up some funds to be used by the partner to market a jointly agreed on activity. Usually these funds are based on revenue and a 3% coop fund is the most widely used practice. A good way of doing this is that both parties finance a campaign 50/50 whereas the manufacturer pays up to 3% of the revenue conducted with that manufacturer. That way both parties have a vested interest in driving the campaign to success.

But there are situations where there simply is no revenue to base a budget on. This happens if either the partner is new or there is a new company, product or service to introduce. In that case we talk about a market development fund or MDF. I have seen everything from $5,000 to $100,000,000 investments.

There is no real rule other than whatever you put in needs to be paid at one point. Typically MDF funds are provided to new partners after a very clear understanding of how the proceeds are to be used or if a new product is introduced and both parties have a good understanding about how much revenue may be generated with the campaign. This is also known as zero based budgeting.

Rules of engagement

Obviously, there are many variations on how to apply the MDF & Coop programs. But here like in any other partner initiative: simplicity is king.

A simple program is more appreciated, more adopted and most importantly more successful than complex rules that have many contingencies and side effects. MDF & Coop programs will not drive or manipulate behavior but enable partners to quickly react to market opportunities and execute.

The most important best practice examples include:

- Provide your partners with at least monthly if not instant online overview of the budget allowance.

- Encourage partners to use the money and match the budget with their own budgets (50/50) engagement.

- Transfer unused Coop Funds (3% of revenue) on a quarterly basis to an MDF fund to help new partners to grow.

- Review the result of each campaign by tracking the leads generated per campaign and their respective closure rate.

- Reward partners who are especially successful and also show what did not work without pointing to the participants.

- Let partners claim their funds as they occur and implement a review process by the channel account partner before it is reviewed by the budget owner.

- Provide a very simple but clear branding guideline on how to use your logo, where to upload it and the same for other images and statements.

- Make it a hard and simple rule: If partners do not use the budget they will not only loose it but also no longer have ANY budget. So you spend it with the active and engaged partners.

- Do not ask for too much with regard to the partner's design capabilities and always keep in mind that the partner is not trying to meet your taste requirements, but to deal with a clientele she knows best.

- Do not let marketing funds degrade and be used for training fees or other expenses. Not only is this a bad practice, it is actually a problem with your compliance committee because the money would be not correctly booked and will be misleading in your reports. Training and education should always be provided for free or managed by a special budgeting process.

3.4. Methodologies for Partner Sales

How to develop a successful external sales force that provides visibility into the sales process and allows influence in critical sales stages

3.5.1   The leading leverage model in sales

3.5.2   Lead Management

3.5.3   Joint Opportunity Management

3.5.4   Guided Selling & Sales Training

3.5.5   Channel -based Forecasting

3.5.6   Channel Sales objectives, goals and metrics

3.4.1. The Leading Leverage Model in Sales

Truly leveraging a channel has very much to do with management structures. The products, partner programs, incentive models, and partner events are important components of channel management but, at this point, has nothing to do with leverage. Channel leverage goes hand in hand with scalability. If you can do all you are doing with and around the channel also with a direct sales force – you are at a non-leveraging model. This model is not scalable and therefore risky when it comes to growth and securing market share.

So look at a channel from the ideal maximum size point-of-view and once you have that defined, work a path to get there. This path will be a dominant element in your long-term channel strategy and the key element in your leverage model. In order to have a model for the discussion, let us assume you have about 100 partners today and a product that should be sold to potentially to about 500,000 companies on a worldwide scale. Your solution costs $10,000 on average and your revenue goal in 5 years from today is to bill $250 million worth of business. To do so you would need to sell it to roughly 25,000 companies. This would represent a 5% market share gain and you may be at roughly 30% market share at this point. If we now apply our 10:1 rule, where you need 1 reseller for every 10 customer you need 2,500 active resellers to sell your product. If you apply the good old 80:20 rule (Pareto) where you do 80% of your business with 20% of your channel you have 500 highly active resellers who do 80% of your business. But in order to identify the 2,500 active resellers you may have to work a 10,000-reseller network to distill the most important partners out of it.

At that scale partner events and incentive models do not count any more. The channel is simply too large. This is where most of the channel organizations collapse and actually even great business models find their limitations, by not being scalable and not being able to leverage large scale channels. *To limit the number of partners is not an option.* Limiting the number of partners results in limited market access, less market share and the potential loss of not only the leadership but even the entire business. This is where smaller companies get bought by bigger ones.

The channel strategy must now be built towards having a potential maximum of 10,000 resellers and you must be able to select and manage about 2,500 active resellers at any given time. If you want to provide datasheets on an ongoing basis to 10,000 resellers, you may have a problem. Providing leads to those resellers may be a problem. Even knowing their sales people and keeping track of sales in constant fluctuation is going to be a problem. Even if you build a typical tree structure to manage countries, territories, groups of channels and then individual channel partners (and reduced overhead to the max) you would still end up having at least one channel salesperson per 30 resellers. With 10,000 potential partners you would need about 330 channel partner managers – way to many - and you would need a decent management structure on top of it. At a channel of that size you need to completely turn your management level 180 degrees.

Rather than you managing groups of resellers, put mechanisms, systems, instruments and methods in place that allow the resellers to manage you as a manufacturer. Rather than you determining every movement of the reseller and controlling it, put a leverage model in place that allows the reseller to comply with those rules and decide to be part of it. Rather than you determining who is your channel partner, let the partners determine whether or not they want to resell and service your product.

With that change in thinking, you need to put measures in place so that enough resellers want to play. You need to build the rules and the method in a way that you manage the number of players by easing the rules so that more and more partners want to join the business. The active ones will be quickly visible within the instruments implemented to monitor channel performance, at the latest, when you review the revenue list.

The change from push to pull, from selecting to being selected, from expressing your interest to having the partner express their interest, is huge. The execution is even bigger. Managing a large-scale channel can only be done by putting highly sophisticated tools in place that allow leveraging the entire channel. If the channel is eventually grown to a big organization but you still work with a small selected group of partners in a 1:1 relationship, the whole channel development effort will probably not pay off.

Large scale channel management systems like modern channel-side enterprise applications may help in accomplishing your management goals but the most important issue is changing the way you think of your channel and the reason for having a large scale channel. If you want to have more partners and simply hope that more partners will give you more revenue, the leveraging effect will not take place. But if either demand or demand generation programs are available to eventually address your total available market, you will need a leverage model that can scale to become the dominant player simply by reaching that market.

Execute on Channel Leverage

As we discussed earlier, the market is huge. You will see a big variety in terms of customer profiles. There are small and big companies, private end-users, non-profit organizations, government, hobbyists, students and all sorts of customers. Some might be more important to you and others may seem to be completely unimportant. However, a market has always a large underlying communication network. People talk to each other, influence each other and may drive a market position from very different angles. You will not want to decide who should and should not be your customer. The prospect decides. Now when it comes to leverage this holds the first opportunity:

Every reseller has its specialty and preference. There are resellers focusing only in large accounts, others deal with mid-size companies. Some resellers play more of an influencer role, while others deal with governments only. Some may just love to work with students and universities and others have no focus at all. Once you decide the marketplace will determine who your customer will be, you may not want to prefer one reseller over the other but let the market itself decide how your product flows into it. Each segment by its own may not be terribly important. However, the sum of all market segments taken together is important. Moreover, the fact that each segment within the entire market is somewhat connected to each other and may exert influence upon each other, this will make a difference.

With a more open channel architecture and less regulations, you will find it easier to manage that channel. It is not less work, but with the same amount of resources, you will be able to drive a bigger channel. Of course, this is only one aspect and one topic in looking at the leverage model. In order to go into the most important topics of the leverage model, we will discuss them piece by piece.

Leveraging Engagement

The larger the channel the more important is a well-thought-through engagement program. If you have the reseller engaged with your company independent of the number of people you have, you have a scalable model and can grow your channel to whatever is the ideal size to cover the entire market. The risk here of course is that the engagement is too personnel-intensive and no other mechanism is in place.

A well-designed channel engagement strategy is built on partnerships with other organizations. Training organizations may be the ones who provide training to your partners rather than you doing it yourself and risking scalability. Other products may work well with your product and you help the resellers to add those to their product line, which keeps the momentum and engagement with you even if the reseller sells other products. Services ideas you develop may be offered to the partners to engage them more.

Keep the engagement in good balance, however. A reseller who is dependent on you is less stable. It must be the reseller's own goal to reduce dependency.

Leveraging the Channel as Competitive Advantage

You will always compete with other manufacturers directly or indirectly. What counts in the end is the number of feet on the street. If you can grow and leverage a large channel, you have a huge competitive advantage – your sales force is simply bigger. If your competitor is a small but highly qualified channel, you will most likely outperform your competitor with your larger sales force. In many cases it is the customer again who looks for choice and availability and if you are not present you have lost the competitive advantage, no matter how good your product is.

Leveraging a Channel

Now let us start from top down. Microsoft claims to have about 800,000 resellers worldwide. Cisco seems to have about 100,000 resellers worldwide. Most of their competitors have a fraction of their market share and a fraction of their channel size. But what was first?

The success model of Compaq in the early days was not only the product, but also the concept of exclusively selling through the channel. No other company in the computer world was able to grow a channel with the speed Compaq did. There were many comparable products, products with more power for a lower price, yet Compaq outperformed those companies. In the end Compaq was the largest PC manufacturer until the mega-flop happened and the company killed itself by destroying its far most valuable asset: its channel. At the same time Cisco put more and more effort into the channel and moved from a direct sales organization to an indirect sales organization. Microsoft early on gave up selling to large companies directly and grew the largest channel organization in the IT world. But no one did it to be able to say, "Look at my huge channel." There is simply one driving force behind their channels: LEVERAGE.

Let us look at the markets in more detail. Assume you have a product that you are going to sell into the mid-market. On a global scale, we have roughly 30 million companies. About 5 million companies are bigger than 100 employees. In order to address the TAM (Total Available Market) you should count a 20:1 ratio, which means you should have 1 reseller for 20 of your target market customers. If your target market within the 5 million companies counts to about 10% or 500,000 companies you should have access to 25,000 resellers. They will not all sell your products on a day-to-day basis, but they give you access to market potential. If you want to be a dominant player in that market, and you know your market, you can rather easily calculate the size of your channel. Going forward it is becoming clearer that the size of the channel cannot be compromised by its quality in order to reach market share. This may sound depressing but the only way to reach the market and its "fair share" is by having complete access to the entire market. Determining the ideal size of the channel comes before the determination of its characteristic and its quality. So many things regarding size have changed, but when it comes to channel, size matters.

If the channel does not perform, it is not the reseller's fault and you prove it wrong by doing it yourself. The true challenge, and your most important job when developing a channel, is to find ways to make your channel perform and reach your entire market segment. At this point, you still may feel that my focus on size relative to quality is not balanced, and quality is much more important to you. I completely understand and appreciate the concern, but look at it from a customer's point of view. What a customer requests and needs and the decision process he undertakes to finally decide for one or the other product, will give you a third perspective. Therefore, you have your perspective, the perspective from your channel partners and many perspectives from many kinds of customers.

Customers Leverage Your Channel Too

How does a customer leverage your channel? Very easily. If she has a choice of buying the product from a retailer, online from a Website, a local reseller, a VAR or a global system integrator, she can choose what she feels is best for her. She may completely know your product, have technical expertise in-house and just wants the product cheap and quick. The customer may also want the product cheap and quick but may have someone to install it for her. The customer may be a global 500 company and want to deploy the product in 30 countries and need respective support. All those scenarios have nothing to do with the complexity of a product but simply with the comfort level a customer may want. As long as you decide what the customer should get, you are better off selling direct and have that direct interaction. If you give the customer the choice, you will want to develop a very diverse channel. Keep in mind, the channel will come to you as long as demand is there, the sales can be made more cost efficient through a channel.

Summary

If your product is channel-ready and so is your organization and you know how big your market is, then you should be able to layout the first step of a channel development plan, which gives you the ideal size of your channel. It also may already give you an indication that this channel will be a mix of different classes of channel organizations. The big questions, however, remain. How do I build it? How do I manage it? How do I maintain and continue to grow it? THE ART OF CHANNEL LEVERAGE will provide you same answers.

3.4.2.   All New Business Starts with a Sales Lead

This section discusses the importance of sales leads. While many people gave up on discussing this matter LEADS IS ALL YOU HAVE TO GENERATE NEW BUSINESS. So not only it is important for your growth but also for your partner's growth. That's why it is one of the most wanted items from partners and why this is the largest chapter in the book.

Synopsis: Don't throw leads over the fence – but collaborate and stay ahead of every single opportunity. Any Dollar you spend in marketing is to generate new sales. If you don't harvest stop any kind of marketing right away and rethink. Distribute hot sales leads of *any* quality to all your partners. Provide quality information and track the follow-up of *every single lead* systematically. Grow lead closure rate through metrics and analysis of lead sources, which will make better performing partners.

Not only are leads one of the top three line items on the partners requirements list, leads are the fuel for sales in general. The partners see themselves as the sales force of the respective manufacturer; they need that fuel. Whether one thinks partners shall generate their own leads or not is a different issue – also important enough to have its own chapter. But whatever the source of the lead, its processing is an art of its own.

As we all know, leads need to be hot. At the same time, many organizations tend to qualify leads to death and still do not get decent results. It's almost like saying" I boil the eggs now for over 20 minutes and they are still not soft"

Leveraging your channel means putting your entire channel behind the leads and let the sales people in the channel follow up with requests rather than expensive and less experienced call centers. Not all the resellers may want unqualified leads, but most of the resellers do not receive any leads at all. Only the top resellers usually receive leads, and they need them the least. Often times, those large reseller organizations do not even have a system for following up with individual sales leads. The smaller resellers will and what is more, they will complain less, they will actually qualify the leads for you, and most likely they will turn more of them into customers.

However, like the whole model of large-scale channel leverage, lead distribution needs the same shift in thinking. Before a sales person assigns any leads to any partner, we need to think WHO is the best partner for those leads and equally important WHO within that partner organization is actually interested in those leads.

But before we go in any details we should group the issues around leads in 3 segments:

- Lead Quality

- Lead Distribution

- Lead Metrics

Lead Quality

Another discussion is around lead quality. This is actually older than lead management itself. Lead quality is one of the most argued topics in any channel conversation. Repeatedly, partners ask for more quality. But what partners are really asking for are orders delivered on a silver platter.

The definition of a quality lead varies greatly depending on the partner who works the lead. Therefore, the key rule to lead qualification is matching. First, matching a lead with a respective partner is more important than any lead pre-qualification activity. Once a match is found, sales people are pushed to close deals fast. This leads to the second most important aspect to lead quality: readiness. If a prospect is ready to buy, the lead is a quality lead in the hands of the right salesperson. Thirdly, the lead needs to be hot, "interested right now," rather than a contact from some weeks ago.

Our finding is that a hot lead (just generated) which is ready to buy (evaluator, influencer and buyer or decision maker), matched up with the best suitable business partner has by far the highest closure rate.

If the qualification process through outsourced call centers takes more than a day or two the "lead temperature" cools down, and the opportunity is already at risk. If the qualification is not at its best possible level, the lead may be qualified as "not interested" and actually be qualified to death. If the hot and interested prospect does not match with the partner, it can be the death of the opportunity as well. All other qualification aspects are nice to have but not critical for closure.

The discussion with resellers, VARs or any kind of business partners about lead quality is a painful and cumbersome conversation with no real results. This has been the case over the last 20 years in almost all industries, worldwide. Resellers ideally want to see perfectly prepared deals where all they need to do is complete an order form and move on. This is a legitimate wish, but has little to do with reality. On the other side, manufacturers throw leads at their partners, asking for quick follow up, without even knowing whether those leads are of any interest to a particular partner. And on top of all this there is no clear definition of lead quality. A high potential customer for one might be a bad lead for someone else. Based on our findings and continuous research to improve the lead management process we put this white paper together and discuss the various aspects of lead quality in detail.

Current Lead Quality Definitions

Today most of the manufacturers who receive sales leads from websites, tradeshows, conferences, mail-responses, advertising or other sources start qualifying the leads before they are given to the sales organizations. During this qualification process, the prospect is asked several questions in order to find out whether the prospect is truly interested:

> "Good morning, my name is Linda Smith and I'm calling on behalf of the XYZ Corporation. How are you this morning Mr. Jones? You recently expressed

interest in the ABC Products of XYZ Corporation. Do you mind if I ask you some questions in order to better provide you with more information?..."

how many qualification calls start like this. And if Mr. Jones is busy and does not want to deal with a call center call, he simply says, "Sorry, but I'm very busy right now and just wanted some information, thanks I'm not really interested right now."

The call center now qualifies the prospect into the "call in 3-6 months" bucket. If the customer makes their decision internally within the next 4 weeks, the prospect is actually qualified to death. There are many other similar scenarios with the same result, but the situation may be even worse. For instance, because the call center is paid on highly qualified A-Leads only, they reach people that actually answer all their questions. Unfortunately, someone who has the time to tell the call center what operating system they have, what kind of Internet provider they use, what ERP system is implemented, etc., is most likely not the decision-maker but rather a person who just enjoys being asked. Closing them is as difficult as getting around them to their supervisor, i.e., decision-maker, to close a deal.

Determining Lead Quality

In order to define quality, it is important to define the results parameter for that quality. With leads, we can make it very simple. The resulting metric is CLOSURE. Nothing is more important when evaluating a lead than its ability to be closed. Other aspects may be of interest but are clearly secondary.

In order to determine lead quality we need to search for factors that guide to a closure of that particular prospect. Currently, most qualifying questions and actions are more distracting than leading us to the goal of closing a prospect. Aspects that really matter:

- **Is it a hot lead**? Was that lead generated within the last few hours? Or is it already cooled down and a few days or even few weeks old?

- **Is the prospect ready to buy** soon (like within your usual sales cycle)? Or is he just looking around to get some ideas, formulate a budget based on that and has no real concept at this point?

- **Is there a matching channel partner** that would be a good fit for that particular business in terms of its capabilities and the size of the deal versus the size of the partner? Or is there no matching partner and closing this deal might be a disappointment for the prospect or the partner?

Any other information about the lead is also nice to have. Of course a salesperson would like to get more information, but all the additional information has nothing to do with the qualifying aspects of closing the prospect. It only has to do with the richness of the information. If the lead quality is defined by the richness of the information, the risk is high that the no.1 qualifying aspect– the lead is hot – is at risk.

I developed the "Lead Cube" which shows the dependencies of each aspect in a visual way.

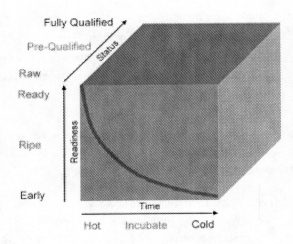

Interesting enough, even if the lead is fully qualified, it does not change the curve, which represents the likelihood of closing the prospect. The qualification certainly adds valuable information to the lead and that is what sales people like to see, but as explained, earlier it takes time away, which is critical in terms of the aging of the lead.

Summary: *The lead quality in respect to "closeability" is overwhelmingly determined by the aging of the lead and by the readiness of the prospect. If this then can be matched with the respective partner, we can state that this partner received a qualified lead.*

Expectations

One of the larger discrepancies with lead quality has to do with the expectation of the partner who receives those leads. Once base definitions are set for what matters and what attributes a lead has, the very next step is to set expectations with the partners very clearly. But first and foremost it is important to agree that the lead is not something for the partner; a lead is followed up and taken care of by an individual salesperson. She needs to understand the concept of lead quality and what the expectations are. Setting the expectations with the wrong people is as problematic as sending the lead to the wrong person.

What a Partner Salesperson Needs to Understand

A sales lead is generated by a certain action from the manufacturer side. This lead represents a prospect that has shown some interest in the product or service. Based on the qualifying data available, the lead is a lead – not an order. If such leads are not interesting to the sales people, they simply should not touch it. The salesperson also should understand that a lead is like a prospect in a department store who is looking for something but has not decided yet. Not everybody who visits a store is also buying. But with the right attitude they may be a purchaser at some point. Finally, it needs to be understood that it is much more resource intensive for the partner's salesperson to do his own cold calling if at the same time he can already receive somewhat interested prospects. Now, if this is not appealing to that salesperson, then he probably is not prospecting at all and is busy with his current engagements, prospects and customers.

In turn, what do you expect? Do you expect a quick follow up with immediate feedback and closure? Probably. Are you able to match up every single lead with the ideal person in the appropriate partner organization? Probably not. Providing your expectations and matching them with your partner's expectations is an absolute *must* in the process of defining lead quality.

Summary: Setting clear expectations with the channel and educating the channel in terms of the value of the leads is an important part of the lead quality process. Quality is always measured against an expectation and measurable values.

When I had a chance to discuss lead management with Angelika Horaitis, VP Global Channels at IBM, it was very impressive to see with what kind of deep analysis sales leads were dissected. The process was developed over a few years but at the end IBM was able to understand where the leads exactly came from, how long it took to distribute to partners and the outcome of each lead. Clearly the more money goes into lead generation the more knowledge you need about its ROI.

Lead Distribution

Managing leads within a direct sales organization is totally different compared to lead management with an indirect organization. While sales organizations in a direct sales environment are well under control and follow company-specific processes, indirect organizations are compiled of hundreds of legally independent companies. There have been many attempts to find the best way of providing leads to partners. One was to simply send the leads to partners, I call it the PUSH methodology. The other was a more intelligent way to let partners pick the leads they are interested in, the PULL methodology. And the last is to neither push or pull leads around but specifically share and collaborate with partners over specific opportunities.

PUSH Methodology

One way to automate lead distribution was to automate the current manual process of sending leads to partners via post, fax or email and automatically sending them through a partner portal. The biggest problem here was that nobody knew if the partner actually followed up or if he even cared. Since this didn't bring good results, a new methodology called PULL was invented and even patented.

PULL Methodology

PULL allowed the reseller sales people to select the leads they wanted. This is an interesting method because it put the partners in the driver seat. Leads were only taken by partners who are really interested in leads. The drawback however was that many leads staled in the system, were never pulled or leads that were pulled by the partner were never followed up and "expired".

SHARE Methodology

This third method is newer and effectively only possible thanks to Internet and the concepts of social networking. Instead of throwing leads over the fence and hoping it will work, this method suggests that the manufacturer keeps ownership of each lead until it is closed or understood that there is just no match between requirement and solution. As this is my suggested method.

But before we decide on any preferred method, let's see what aspects we should look at

Lead Readiness

Finding out whether a decision is to be made soon or will take a while is, again, one of the very important questions that make a salesperson tick. If a decision to purchase is coming soon, a salesperson needs to be in touch with the prospect right away. If a purchase decision is not planned right now, sales people or anybody else will incubate that lead for a while. In order to find out, the prospect simply needs to be asked. This can be easily done on the website, it can be asked at marketing response elements, it can be asked at a seminar or tradeshow floor and it can be asked at any other event. We believe it is important to ask only that question rather than gather any other additional information. By providing a multiple-choice check box, you can narrow it down to 1 of 4 options:

- Is it within X amount of time? (X represents the span of your typical sales cycle)

- Is it within 2-3 X? (So you know it is on the horizon but not really very short term.)

- It is not really budgeted yet.

- It is not in my responsibility.

If one of the first two answers is given plus the fourth, a salesperson knows there is something going on, but the prospect is not the right person. If only option 4 is checked, it means that there is an interest, but a budget is not known and this is not the right person to evaluate this opportunity. It is however, enough information to qualify the readiness of that prospect. Of course, there are many people who just do not want to disclose any information. This is usually due to one of the following reasons:

- The prospect wants to deal with somebody in person rather than with a Website or piece of paper – even more reason to follow up personally.

- The prospect does not want to be bothered while evaluating various options. She wants to take her time and then decide. This is a critical case where it is necessary to be present without upsetting the prospect.

- The prospect has already made up his mind and is just looking for arguments to prove his decision. There is still some chance that a good salesperson can turn this situation to her best interest.

All in all, it always comes back to readiness, timing and the ability to influence the decision.

Lead Follow-Up

If the prospect is ready, nothing is more important than being present. The risk of being too late outweighs the risk of being too early by an order of magnitude. In particular, with products where a decision phase can be as short as a few days or weeks, providing leads for follow up in a month is a deadly exercise. Even with deals that have a several month sales cycle, it is very frustrating to wait a few days or even weeks for a manufacturer response. Sometimes even sales people think that a quick follow up is a treat to a prospect. Taking care and offering help is usually a courtesy and very well received by a prospect. Sales leads from any source should be in the hands of a sales-professional within a matter of hours or at the most one or two days. Any longer period poses a huge risk of losing the opportunity to influence the decision.

Lead Matching

Matching a lead to a respective partner's salesperson is probably the single most important part in the qualification process. At the same time, it seems almost impossible. As the number of incoming leads increases, the matching needs to be system-based rather than manual or by attempting to automate inefficient manual processes. One of the limiting factors of lead matching is the scalability of methods or processes in place. Today the manufacturer-side sales team wants to be in charge and decide who should get which lead. This is the biggest failure of all in lead management and qualification systems. There are smaller partners and bigger partners, partners with more or less revenue, partners with different skill sets and partners with different motivation to follow up with new sales leads. Even if one partner's salesperson seems to be ideal today, he might be in a project tomorrow and less ideal to follow up with leads. People change responsibilities and people have their own schedules. Last but not least, people are on vacation or on business trips and may not always be available. Still a prospect is a person with an interest that needs to be matched with the best possible salesperson in order to increase the chances of closing a deal.

After countless attempts to identify matching patterns and a mechanism to catch all the various options, we concluded that the salesperson within the reseller organization is herself best suited to select her own leads. She knows best if she can take the responsibility of a certain lead and follow up based on her own immediate availability, interest to go after new opportunities, and commitment to process the lead and turn it into a customer. With this thought we not only get the job done, we leverage the entire channel and by definition make sure that an ever-changing channel has a natural selection process: Only the available and hungry sales people will go after the fresh leads.

By moving away from pushing leads out and instead having partners pull the leads, we have achieved one of the biggest steps in improving lead quality. By using the pull method, the remaining qualification aspects were easy to cover. Leads are matched with partners by geography and product authorization, if needed. This means that sales people can choose only leads, which match their profile.

However, as good as the lead distribution by PULL looks on paper, it has its mayor flaws. The cherry picking that we knew from the old push model is also happening in the PULL model. As we explained earlier, PULL still doesn't give anybody control and visibility into the process and at the end we experienced a lot of stale leads in the system as well as leads that were pulled but not really followed up. I came to realization that the problem is not the method of LEAD DISTRIBUTION but LEAD DISTRIBUTION itself.

So before we look any further, let's understand some more aspects of lead management such as lead quantity, geographic spread, leads per partner and territory and make a decision of best practices in lead management once we have the complete picture. One element is coverage. As we discussed coverage models before, it is recommended to review partner coverage by channel type to ensure that there are actually partners to work on the leads.

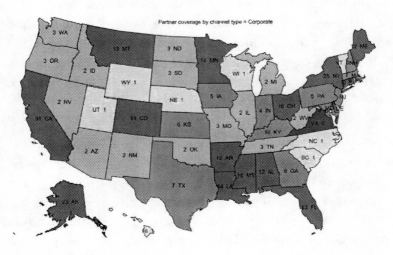

Coverage report

This report allows manufacturers to visualize their partner coverage, by channel type, for a given geography. This example shows a state with no coverage.

Another report could be generated that shows the generated leads by territory for the top 10 territories.

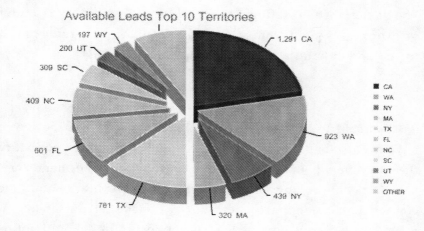

This report visualizes the number of available leads for each of the top 10 revenue producing territories.

The perfect report is to visualize the number of partners per territory and right next to it the number of leads generated.

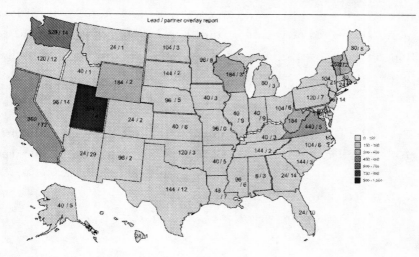

The "Lead/Partner Ration Report" shows if a territory is under or over represented from a lead point of view. This report need to go hand in hand with the partner type reporting.

All that said I came to the realization that Lead Distribution in any way or shape is not working effectively enough to justify the investment in generating the leads on one hand and securing enough growth for the business on the other hand. The complexity is not the process but the fact that ownership of expensively generated new leads or opportunities should not be distributed. Instead I suggest that whoever invests into new business opportunities and generates new leads should keep ownership and control until the lead is either closed or it is understood that there is no deal. More so as the creator of the lead jointly works such opportunities with their partners, there is a much better understanding about lead quality, lead follow up process and sales cycles versus just handing them over. I would not accept an argument that it is too costly for a manufacturer to be involved and therefore the partner has to do that on their own. If that is truly the case, how can a partner make money by performing the whole sales process if it is too costly to just look at it and accompany the partner.

Channel Excellence Methodology suggests that you consistently share your leads with the partners in a way that the partner may work through the sales process and be the main point of contact for the customer but the manufacturers sales team should be completely aware of the status and progress of any lead in the pipe.

3.4.3.   Deal Registration Programs

One critical technique to get a better picture about the partner's opportunities is to ask partners to register their deals. In turn an important practice for partners is to 'secure' deals and effort by registering them with the respective manufacturer to make sure the manufacturer does not compete with the partner.

> **Synopsis**: Deal registration is a key program for both partner and manufacturer to increase the probability of winning an opportunity. It has reached high visibility that even antitrust laws reviewed the practice. While the intention to focus and alleviate friction between partners, there is also a negative flavor of control of the market. But deal registration programs are mainly to increase the understanding of deals under partners.

The single most important aspect of deal registration is channel conflict reduction or elimination. Deal registration shall not be used to control the deal flow in the channel and regulate an otherwise free market. There is however a very fine line. Often times manufacturers have only limited resources and just cannot engage with multiple partners on a specific deal. In other cases manufacturers need to motivate the smaller partners to continue their costly presales phase against so called volume dealers who at the end of the sales cycle break in a deal and sell with a better price. So we decided to develop two types of deal registration programs, one with and another with no financial advantage but just support. We realized that even with no financial support but only an active and joint sales engagement is motivation enough to join a program. Additional sales incentives range from 0.5% extra discount for a registered deal all the way up to 20% extra discount. The financial motivation may be high and the legal conflict may be growing with the size of the extra discount. But over time the industry and also justice understands that presales efforts need to be supported and nobody can expect a company to succeed by providing equal discount for non equal engagement.

SEVEN SECRETS FOR SUCCESS

There is one primary issues in indirect business for which sophisticated deal registration systems provide a great solution: Supporting the investment in prospects with longer sales cycles, and protecting the partner's engagement against potential channel conflicts.

Utilizing the following Seven Secrets will help ensure a successful deal registration program that drives significant channel business growth.

1. Understand the partner's perspective

For many channel partners, the growing popularity of deal registration programs is forcing them to weigh the benefits of participation (e.g., pricing incentives) against the cost of internal resources required to administer participation. Because program success will be directly correlated to partner adoption, manufacturers should carefully consider the partner's perspective and automate as much of the process as possible.

Manufacturers should also provide partners with the ability to track registration status online in real-time. This will reduce inefficient status check phone calls and emails, benefiting both parties with reduced program support and administration costs.

2. Align the program with corporate objectives

I mentioned that over and over already but also here, understanding how key program elements can drive the partner behavior required to help the company achieve its overall goals and objectives is essential. Deal registration program elements fall into five general categories:

Eligible Products.   Focus on the products and services that best support overall corporate objectives. If a manufacturer needs to jumpstart market share for a new product introduction, then the program should allow registrations of new-product deals and incentives should offset partner investments to come up to speed on the latest technology. Conversely, if maintaining market share for well-established low-margin products is a goal, then the program should reward loyal partners by providing margin relief.

Deal Size: Establish a minimum revenue amount for eligible deals.

Disclosure.   Establish a minimum number of days prior to closure that a deal must be registered in order to be eligible, and reward disclosure behavior accordingly. If a manufacturer requires improved channel revenue predictability, then the program incentives should be skewed to reward partners for disclosing deals earlier in the sales cycle.

Closure.   Establish a maximum number of days during which the deal must close in order to be eligible for incentives. Select a closure timeframe that is realistic yet provides incentive to get the deal done. If a typical sales cycle is 90 days, consider setting the closure threshold at 120 days to provide partners with a reasonable cushion.

Eligible Partners.   Establish partner eligibility criteria that are aligned with the other elements of the program, specifically product or market mix and deal size.

3. Provide privacy protection for unapproved deals

Many deal registration programs fail because the most important partners refuse to register hot and strategic deals. The crown jewels for any partner are its customer and prospect data. If the partner registers the data, they are exposed. If they don't, the manufacturer is unable to decide whether or not to approve the registration.

Breaking this stalemate requires both sides to give a little. Partners must be able to register deals with a high degree of confidentiality. If the manufacturer approves the registration, detailed information is exposed. However, if the manufacturer does not approve the registration, the details remain confidential and the privacy of the deal is protected.

4. Publish and enforce the program rules

Of all the factors critical to the success of a deal registration program, effective communication and consistent enforcement of program rules may top the list. Manufacturers must create simple, clear criteria for deal registration submissions and approvals. This information must be published and supporting processes must be put in place to ensure the rules are well enforced. The rules should be communicated within the context of the registration process to avoid misunderstandings.

5. Automate and integrate the process

Many deal registration programs fail because only one part of the process has been automated – registration. The follow on of such registered deals kind of evaporate in the day to day hectic. Partners ask: why register in the first place. Therefore deal registration programs need to define the full deal life cycle from start to finish. All participants need to have clarity over that process. The key elements should include registration – review – approval/rejection with confirmation - joint collaboration or at least knowledge of the progress – closure with feedback whether successful or not and why.

6. Identify deals in critical sales stages

One key component of a successful deal registration program is providing partners with sales assistance to win the business. The ability to quickly identify strategic opportunities in critical phases of the sales cycle will enable both parties to collaborate efficiently and allocate resources properly. Automating and integrating the end-to-end process is the first step. Next, manufacturers must provide partners with an easy way to keep deal status up to date. If the update process is too difficult or resource intensive for the partner, deal status will grow stale and the program will not be operating at optimum effectiveness. Practice showed that partners are not going back to a manufacturer provided system to provide feedback. Therefore it is essential to the success of a program that partners and manufacturers can collaborate in a networked environment.

7. Measure, review and improve.

The last, but certainly not the least, success factor is program measurement.

Optimizing program performance requires a closed loop of timely, accurate and meaningful information. Manufacturers must have a mechanism in place to track program performance in a timely fashion, ideally real-time.

These Seven Secrets are the crucial elements to building deal registration programs that are mutually-beneficial for both the manufacturer and the reseller.

Given the discount incentive is easy to understand and follow, I'd like to present a deal registration program with no financial incentive:

EXAMPLE

----

1)   Acme Deal Registration Program

This deal registration program applies to all authorized Acme Partners, regardless of size or location. The purpose of the program is to provide Acme with a better insight in partner's sales opportunities for a better planning process of Acme Corp. The program shall in turn provide partner with a better understanding of the sales support they receive and alleviate channel conflict between the Acme sales force and the partner's sales force.

2)   Opportunity Registration Program Terms

a.   A partner opportunity must be registered through the web based Acme Deal Registration System.

b.   Acme provides the privacy protection feature. Unless a deal is approved, Acme has no visibility into the registration details such as contact names, phone numbers, email addresses.

c.   The Approval process takes typically no more than 1 business day.

d.   Once the opportunity is approved, the partner has full support of the Acme sales force, who will help as a resource to close a deal. If a registered deal is not closed within 6 month, the deal registration expires automatically and with no specific communication.

e.   If the opportunity is rejected, the partner will still be able to work the opportunity but Acme will not provide any support to close the opportunity.

3)   Opportunity Specification

a.   To register a deal, a defined initiative at a defined customer location with a respective name of a project leader needs to be registered.

b.   A registration that is identified as immature (no real business opportunity can be identified) will be canceled by Acme. If the business environment changes, it can be re-registered.

c.   Other opportunities outside the specified location or department will not be covered by the opportunity registration process.

d.   The Acme Deal Registration System also requires a minimum opportunity size, as well as a maximum closure time range.

4)   Account Management

a.   Once an opportunity is registered and approved, Acme will neither approve nor support a competing opportunity registration from other partners. Instead focus its efforts to jointly win the opportunity with the registering partner.

b.   The registered account will be managed by the respective partner with full support from the Acme sales and service team

c.   Acme does neither charge partner nor reduce fees for any of the support effort Acme may provide to help close an opportunity.

5)   Acme Named Accounts

a.   Acme conducts business with a series of direct accounts including the existing accounts.

b.   Acme manages its named accounts in a system so a registration for an account that already is an Acme account will automatically be rejected by the system. If the partner wishes to collaborate with Acme on such accounts, an individual arrangement should be made. Acme is very open to collaborate with its partners in such accounts.

6)   Exceptions

a.   Opportunities that are outside the Opportunity Registration Program Framework (timeline or price range) need to be discussed and negotiated with Acme and require written approval.

b.   Acme may jointly work with partners on Acme' named accounts. In this case a commission may be paid if there is a corresponding written agreement. A verbal agreement or any verbal expectations from either party will not be acceptable.

The above example demonstrates how partners and manufacturers collaborate in certain deal and clearly alleviates channel conflicts for those registered cases. Anxiety from the partner side that a manufacturer may not conform to such rules is extremely low as a breach of those rules would only happen once.

Channel Excellence Methodology suggests that deal registration programs need to carefully crafted to eliminate the risk of market control and legal issues. But deal registration is an important factor in gaining trust with partners and ensuring that all participants have a good understanding about opportunity ownership and margin distribution. A well defined deal registration program is one of the most important contributors to alleviate channel conflict. It is not so much the content itself but more importantly the fact that a program is in place.

Joint Opportunity Management

This section discusses how the most successful manufacturers in High Tech work with their partners and collaborate over joint business opportunities. It is the natural extension of the previous chapter where we talked about leads but now explores the joint opportunity process and its potential for all types of alliances. While Leads was the largest chapter, Joint Opportunity Management is probably the most important when it comes to actually managing the sale.

Synopsis: Sharing is a key characteristic of the evolution of human beings. We learned to share knowledge, wealth and information and realized that sharing actually brings more than keeping it for you. Sharing opportunities with others and create a joint success is more successful over time than keeping everything for yourself. Opportunity sharing is NOT an act of charity, but a method to higher profitability.

We learned in the previous chapter that lead distribution was never really successful but collaborating with partners made companies like Cisco to clear leaders in their industry. One sided opportunity management had its times but in days where the business world is entirely networked, we can no longer think in a one dimensional hierarchy. What I mean with that sentence is that not only we are networked with our partners, but in turn they are networked with their peers and alliances and other manufacturers who sometimes live in competition with us. A business opportunity unless it is a consumer good is most of the times a web of solutions itself. If a customer is buying new software, most of the times there is also a purchase of new hardware involved. And while partners more and more specialize in certain areas, they create bonds with peers to ensure they can deliver a complete solution. See also the Peer-to-Peer Business chapter.

When I spoke to many sales leaders and it came to opportunity sharing I noticed an immediate shock. Some just waiting what I have to say, others immediately overrunning me with the question: "Why on earth should I share any opportunity with anybody?" This was probably the most common reaction. And the more channels savvy somebody was the more open they were to hear my opinion.

Sharing opportunities is what direct sales does every time and always. The sales manager shares the opportunities with his team and they work the opportunity while the manager is always up to date with what happens in those opportunities. If it is a good manager he or she only steps in if something doesn't sound right. Otherwise the sales person handles the deal. This is no different than the ideal picture of a channel sales manager. The channel sales manager knows every opportunity of her partners and only steps in if something is not right or the partner needs help. The dilemma however is that so far partners and manufacturers did not share any system that allowed both groups to monitor a deal without always calling them and checking if everything is OK. Some did and partners quickly got annoyed. Others didn't and the deals went south without notice.

Like we explored in the Leads chapter: Throwing opportunities over the fence is dangerous and not very likely to be successful. The biggest challenge here is not so much the willingness of sharing but the actual tools to be able to monitor the progress of such opportunities. The current PRM systems, partner portals or opportunity management systems have all one major flaw: It is a point to point relationship between a partner and a manufacturer. But the channel is a networked world and not a hierarchical structure. Partners work with 30 manufacturers on average and there is no way to update 30 different systems with every change of an opportunity.

I remember a very interesting conversation with Stephan Rossius, VP worldwide Partners at SAP. His vision was to build a product that provided partners the ability to collaborate in large complex projects while SAP and all participating partners would be able to keep track of the progress. The sheer complexity of the project took him years to develop. The major problem again was also here that partners would connect to SAP to work their projects at SAP, knowing that they had to replicate the effort in their own system. Stephan has retired and to my knowledge the project was ceased. But it was a very influential meeting to my later work at Xeequa. Leveraging the Internet and dramatically simplifying processes enabled us to realize Stephan's dreams in a different way. We built independent nodes where every reseller OWNES their piece of the network and therefore doesn't need to replicate the effort. More so they can share the opportunity with peers and other complementary vendors to increase their success rate. See peer-to-peer networking in the next chapter.

The biggest issue raised by partners in the US and Europe was the lack of networking capabilities. When I talked to partners and went into more details, they had a hard time to work with all the different manufacturer systems out there. One reseller said:"I really like to work with most my manufacturer partners, but the one thing I hate is that they degrade their partner portal to a 'branding experience'. I know the brand and I'm committed. All I need is information fast and don't want to go through training to leverage their deal registration system. Ideally I register a deal in MY SYSTEM and somehow magically it moves in whatever system they use. When I talked to some engineers to build such a system they said: "That will never happen. You can't connect everybody with everybody – that is way too complicated and will never get ready, let alone the updates."

Well, but the need was obvious and the problem is getting rather bigger than smaller. So I decided to give it a try. And rather integrating everything with everything I choose to create a system that is simply an autonomous network, where every participant owns its node and connect to everybody they like and trust.

At that stage it became very apparent to me that the lack of collaboration between partners and their manufacturers is not so much a lack of understanding, a lack of discipline, trust or methodology, it is simply a lack of technology. And while we all talk about partner networks and a networked world, many still view the relationship between manufacturer and partner a point to point relationship, while in reality is a interwoven network of connections between partners, their manufacturers, their peers and other alliances and exactly that happens in each node of that global business network.

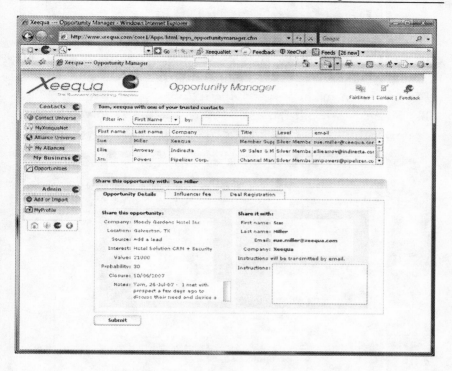

Screenshot of the opportunity sharing process

When you share an opportunity in Xeequa for instance, you select somebody from within your trusted network. That person will find the opportunity in HIS or HER system. As everybody in Xeequa has an autonomous node, they can share the opportunity with people they have in their trusted network. This may be for many people a huge leap of faith in their partners but on the other hand partners always share information with peers they trust but manufacturers never knew it nor did you have an idea who those other people were.

A good system actually shows you all the participating parties in such opportunities. In the screenshot below you see an example where a specific opportunity is shared with others. The line item in the upper table is the opportunity. The little list is the list of partners or people who are involved in that opportunity. As you click on a contact in that list you get the

details such as name, company name, phone number and email address. On the right hand side you see the comment and status information from that partner / person.

In this example the manufacturer or partner (it doesn't matter) has full insight into the team composition of the opportunity. He may meet people or companies he otherwise has never heard of. This is the effect of a true network. This also makes a bid clearer why so many companies look at social media and how social networks can help them better network in a fully networked world.

That is interestingly enough the point of convergence, where networked applications may replace many older tools that were designed to administrate and maintain captured data in an inhouse, behind the firewall application. Also the development in peer-to-peer business as explained in the next chapter is a sign of the development of our networked world.

Channel Excellence Methodology suggests that you invest a great deal of time in understanding the composition of your deals relative to other suppliers and how you can win deals in collaboration with your partners and alliances in the most effective way. Share your opportunities with partners and encourage your partners to share the opportunity with other partners who may be important and complementary to close the deal. Take the spirit of alliances a step farther and lead by leveraging even your partner's partners.

3.4.4.   Peer to Peer Networking

This very short section is just touching on an interesting development in indirect channels, the business between partners. Peer to Peer Business has grown dramatically in the last few years.

> **Synopsis**: Be aware of the fact that the business between partners is rapidly growing. It has become a multi Billion $ market and is not the business of selling each other excess inventory but complementing deals and engaging each other to the benefit of the joint customer.

I recently spoke with the president of a large Microsoft partner alliance and he mentioned that this group traded business worth of about $6Billion in 2006. While still small relative to the Trillion Dollar IT industry it shows a dramatic change in regards to partner cooperation, business networking and alliances that more and more ignore the fact that there may be some flavor of completion involved as well.

I will explore much more details in my new book "Business Networking Excellence" but wanted to mention this as one of the most important trends in channel management. There is a reason that John Chambers, CEO of Cisco encourages their partners to collaborate more. The peer to peer collaboration is beneficial for all parties. Manufacturers gain access to complementary partner groups, increase their network value and increase their marketing reach. Partners in turn can focus on their core competency and winning a deal with other competent partners who don't hope to do it all. And the customer wins because he gets a group of highly competent specialists instead of a generalist and at the same time may continue working with one partner who just transparently pulls in his peers.

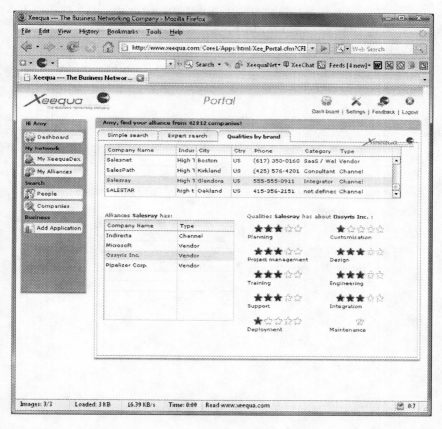

The screenshot above makes a bid clearer how the power of per-to-peer relationships will be used on the future.

You may select a partner from the upper table. As you select the partner the smaller list on the lower left hand side shows the partners they work with. Once you click on any of those peers or manufacturers the qualities chart shows what kind of services the partner offers by brand.

Examples like that demonstrate the power of the networked world. If a consumer or corporate buyer is trying to look for a local partner that has experience in Cisco, HP and Symantec and offers implementation for all three brands and training for Cisco, that search would be a never ending journey. But in the above example a partner is exposing their respective qualities and the search engine matches the requirements with the available data.

Channel Excellence Methodology suggests that you better understand the partners your partners are collaborating with and actually encourage your partners to leverage other partners in opportunities. One way to lead that development is that you actually develop a network of complementary partners and actually introduce them to your selling partners on a deal by deal situation.

3.4.5.   Guided Selling & Sales Training

This section discusses the need for training from two perspectives, the channel side and the manufacturer side. It also provides a view in areas where training may be requested but not needed, discussing who should invest in the trainings and how this investment can be amortized. Finally, it compares partner education with employee education.

Synopsis: No matter what was tried in the last 50 years, it seemed almost impossible to involve sales people in sales training and at the same time the most wanted support from sales people is training. This is not an oxymoron but a problem in processes. Provide contextual training where an when it is needed most directly -- in the sales process.

Channel partner training will be divided into three parts: sales training, training for customer support and training for engineering of any kind. Training will vary by product and service type, but it will help to encapsulate the training issue and solve the problem on a macro level first.

We have studied many partners and many manufacturers and we always come to one conflicting situation: Sales people want training; manufacturers want to train sales people, but it never seems to happened. By diving deeper we have discovered the problem is really timing. A sales person is selling and does not take too much time for education. However, if there is a deal where he needs the knowledge, he is absolutely willing to get training. The problem is that at that very moment no training is available. Online training has been a big step in the right direction, but the overwhelming number of trainings and the complexity of the sales situations did not really synch up without a system in place.

We created what we call "Guided Selling". Selling is clearly a very individual process, but the required knowledge can be captured as a pattern. The pattern is the product one sells. So we suggested providing sales tips for each product right with the lead that is distributed to the partner. So if the lead is based on a request for Server-X, why not send all key information with that lead. For instance, we include a link for online training, the value proposition, how to compete against other competitors, leadership aspects (price leader, functionality lead, availability lead etc.), the most important sales tips and other sales-relevant information.

Once we put that in place in conjunction with an online lead distribution system, we received great feedback from partners. Garth stated, "...that alone is reason for me to pick up leads and follow up with them."

We also learned that a link to technical specifications is much more important than the specification itself. Sales people have their own rhythm of selling and technical sales is clearly not the first thing they think of.

After having that system in the field, we realized how difficult it is for most manufacturers to generate a simple and useful value proposition. What is discussed and decided in the internal direct sales team stays within that team and is not shared with the channel – hence the channel seems to be again at a disadvantage.

Any sales tips that were provided seemed to come from channel sales or marketing administrative assistants. Getting the management team to decide what value proposition a partner sales person should communicate became very cumbersome. Again, this demonstrates how important it is to actually have a channel strategy with all its aspect in place.

However, guided selling does not replace a good sales training, but at least it helps all channel sales people move a great deal forward.

Channel Excellence Methodology suggests that you support your partner's sales teams as well as your own. Instead of continuous local education, provide the partner's sales teams with the most important information to successfully sell your products or services: value proposition, competitive advantage, competitive intelligence, selling aids, pricing, service advantage and other information that helps close a deal.

3.4.6.   Channel-based Forecasting

This section discusses how channel sales organizations do forecasting and why forecasts from the channel are rather tricky.

> Synopsis: As sales are conducted by hundreds or thousands of legally independent companies, consolidating all those forecasts is a real challenge. In order to actually get channel-based forecasts, new methodologies and reporting systems need to be implemented.

Reseller, VAR, broker, dealer: All have their own way of planning their business. In very many cases, a sales forecast is not part of their planning principles. As manufacturers are in need of a forecast to plan production and development, an indirect channel may be an unexpected challenge. Two things need to be understood: 1) Manufacturers who work with channels for more than 10 years pretty much gave up requesting partners to provide forecasts but rather do their own estimation based on market trends and historic data points. 2) As reporting is becoming increasingly important not only for production and internal financial planning but also for external financial reporting, we no longer can shake our shoulders and simply do without a robust forecast.

Having a controllers diploma (I felt I would need it once), helped me better design many financial processes and also gave me the necessary basis to develop a new and disruptive forecast methodology. It was very clear to me that asking 10,000 partners and their 50,000+ sales people to provide me with reports that I can consolidate, while they would need to provide other manufacturers with different forecasts would be an impossible task. To reduce the channel just to satisfy my planning needs was not an option either. So we had to actually create a new methodology that would work for us, but also for pretty much every other manufacturer. So we looked for the most common data points and for simple processes to actually get those data points.

The data points are: 1) estimated revenue, 2) probability and 3) estimated closure. The revenue piece is rather simple but the judgment for probability and estimated close expectations have a spread that could not be bigger between all sorts of partners. Analyzing the actual events behind each of the sales processes and an ability to track and measure them became the most important part of it. As a manufacturer, we should know what it takes to sell a product in an average sales cycle. And we should know how each of the steps affects the probability of closure. We should also know how long it takes from one step to the other, and when a closure could be expected – at least on average.

Now rather than asking people, "What they think is the probability of winning a deal?" We started to ask, "Where are you in the process, and which steps are completed?" By dramatically simplifying and at the same time unifying the various sales process to 7 steps or less, forecasting is getting a new quality. Of course some of the sales processes are different than others, some of the steps take more time than others based on the product and target group, but can a partner sales person differentiate the variations of a sales process between 100 different products from 20 different manufacturers? Not very likely. Over time I reduced the variations und number of sales process steps to these 6 and realized they work if one sells a car, a computer, a house, an insurance policy or just a cell phone:

1) Identifying interest, budget situation, timeline

2) Understanding needs and requirements

3) Working on a solution, referencing successes

4) Demoing, testing, trials

5) Final term negotiation

6) Closing the deal

Now if you can assign a probability by process step like Step1 means a 5% closure probability but if you are at step 5 you are at 90% and do that across the product line, you have a much better understanding of your forecast as if you check with any sales person who may interpret each step differently.

So rather than having a chit chat based forecast like "Hey what do you think?" – "Man not sure but may be 50% - is that good for you?" Take processes and methods and calculate the forecast for yourself.

Channel Excellence Methodology suggests that you move from a forecast "by conversation" to a more methodological forecast and simplify the underlying process and unify the forecast algorithm across product lines.

3.4.7.   Channel Sales Analysis

This section discusses various ways to develop key performance indicators for the sales organization.

> **Synopsis**: Given that new channel management technologies are available and provide lots of data, executive managers still must decide how to manage new channels with specific data points, what kind of metrics can be used and how this all flows into a channel management process which helps drive better results and improves the return on channel investment.

Channel Side Sales Cycles

Analyzing the sales cycles throughout an indirect sales channel seems to be an impossible task. Every partner has its own methodology of selling, its own system of reporting sales and its own way of tracking its effectiveness. In addition, there is the problem of reducing the time from generating leads at the manufacturer side to actually distributing those leads to partners. The whole process is geographically dispersed and its resources are branched out very far – sometimes with distributors in between, completely invisible to a manufacturer. Getting meaningful sales cycle information from indirect sales organizations seems to be impossible – therefore people may even declare it as useless.

It would help to know how long things take in order to find situations you may want to improve. It would be interesting to be able to compare various channel partners in terms of their respective sales cycles, so that you can train others to improve. You want to be able to compare your competitor's selling speed maybe to your organization's. Would not this be a mission critical piece of information that would allow you to shorten your sales cycle by, say, 10 percent, which translates to a higher revenue stream?

Knowing your sales cycle is one of the most important data points to manage your sales. It helps you fine-tune the processes, which on the sales side is always a double trigger: More revenue and less cost. If you know what takes the longest in your selling process, you may be able to shorten exactly that part of the process. If you know at what point of the process you lose most of your deals, you can specifically focus on that part of the process. Solutions will begin appear on the surface. PRM solutions will begin to be developed to help better understand your channel. Lead Management solutions will appear to faster distribute sales leads. It still does not solve the transparency issue with the channel, but all of that was a good first step in the right direction.

Usually a sales cycle starts with a raw, unqualified contact. A typical process today looks like the following scenario:

STEP – 1

A contact is developed from any kind of marketing campaign, like a mail shot, tradeshow, web visit or similar action. This and other contacts will be aggregated at some point and given to an organization internally or externally to pre-qualify. Depending on the feedback this contact is then handed to a salesperson, or—if no immediate interest was identified—the contact is stored in a database for further penetration. We identified the following Top 5 risks in this early stage of contact:

▶ **Risk No.1**—The call center who qualified the lead was not getting to the person and therefore qualified the lead to death. (No interest).

▶ **Risk No.2**—The prospect simply did not want to talk to the call center people and expressed "No Interest." Again, the lead is dead.

▶ **Risk No.3**—The prospect could not articulate his real interest, and the call center mis-qualified the prospect.

▶ **Risk No.4**—The call center takes too long to get to the prospect, and the prospect took another offer.

▶ **Risk No. 5**—The call center does not come as across in a very professional manner, and the prospect is put off so buys somewhere else.

As the reader can see, we identified a misbehavior by qualifying prospects to death, before a salesperson even had a chance to get in touch with the prospect. Of course, many sales people only want to go after highly qualified leads. The reason is very clear; they are *fortunately* busy with other prospects and customers. However, there are always sales people out in the channel who are hungry for new contacts and willing to follow up on even raw, unqualified leads. The only way to satisfy both resources is to ask them and instantiate a process that supports both groups. If you and your teams shares leads or opportunities with the respective group of partners, they know by profile and connection what to do when.

STEP – 2

Now a sales lead (qualified or not) is shared with a reseller. In many cases, this is a manual process. The lead is given to channel sales people who then give it further to the regional channel managers who take care of their partners. Sometimes the leads are automatically assigned to a partner and sent by e-mail, other times the lead is actually physical delivered to the reseller. If we say reseller, of course, it is our main contact at that reseller company. Even so, the lead may be automatically delivered by a lead management system – from now on the lead travels manually within the reseller organization. Depending on whether the best matching person is in the office or not, busy or not and other criteria, the lead will be routed further – or not. It may take days for the lead to reach the actual salesperson, who will then try to contact the prospect. We all know that many of the leads never even make it to salesperson.

So instead of distributing it and hoping it will work, well networked sales people just share it directly with the person they know and begin to engage right away.

Now GTA (Generated to Action) gives you the time, from when a lead was generated in the first place until a salesperson actually starts contacting the prospect.

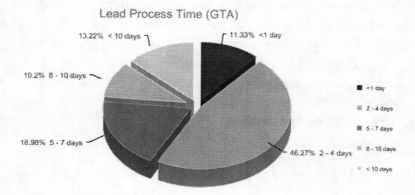

Measuring this is of outmost importance. I was involved in a large project inside a big Networking Manufacturer where we realized that the average GTA was 14 days. That was too long. But the most devastating figure had yet to come: The average sales cycle was 14 days. That means that the competition already satisfied the customer's needs while this company was still figuring out who should get the leads within their chain.

You may know your sales cycle. But if you don't know your GTA I'd say you are in deep trouble.

STEP – 3

Now the real sales process begins. The designated salesperson in the reseller organization starts contacting the prospect in person and identifies her needs as well as identifies a sales opportunity. This is an important point in the sales process, because it is an early flag for a go or no go, not so much a lead qualification but a deal qualification. For a sales cycle analysis it is important to know when this first contact happened and the first feedback for that particular lead was reported. As long as the manufacturer's partner manager is aware of the process, you are in good shape. But if you are not, risk increases that the sales person on the partner side looses focus or works on some easier deals.

STEP – 4

Once the initial contact is made selling begins. Very much depending on products, services and relations, the sales process can be divided in numerous steps until a deal is closed or lost. The sales process may be as short as another call to get an order or may be several month of setting up meetings, reviewing needs and solutions, preparing demos and prototypes, evaluating and testing products, deploying pilot implementations and eventually win or lose such a project. Several years ago I asked a channel manager from Cisco: If you really sell almost all the deals through the channel, why do you have such an enormous sales force? The answer was crisp and to the point: "Because we want to make sure that every customer understands the value of Cisco, therefore we accompany our partners on almost all deals". The result speaks for itself. And if one has the luck to look behind the scene, the Cisco channel managers mange hundreds of deals while their direct selling completion can't handle much more than 20 or 30.

STEP – 5

After the last steps in the sales process and the deal is closed the review phase comes where you review lead or opportunity sources, sales cycle and many other obvious metrics to later on improve the sales process. This could easily fill a whole chapter but since I'm not trying to teach sales processes but focus on the channel aspect I'd like to point you to one report: Lead closure by quality. It is very interesting to review how the "raw leads" actually close in relationship to the highly qualified "A Leads".

Lead Closure By Quality Index

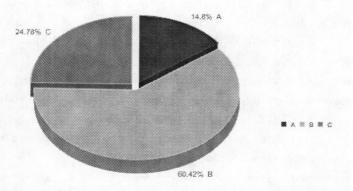

This report shows the lead closure rate based on the quality of the lead. This example shows that it may well be that "highly qualified A Leads" actually contribute less than the more average B-Leads to the result.

How to get the Data Points

Now since we know what we should know and how valuable this information would be, the question remains how to get these data without spending additional resources to gather all these data points and information and without interrupting the sales process. One solution is to engage telemarketing organizations, which follow up with channel partners and find out what the processes and the results look like. However, this gives either just sample information or is extremely expensive.

BlueRoads developed a system that manages the full lead life cycle from generation of a lead to its completion (closed or lost). In order to make it extremely easy for sales people to report that information, the system works on all the sales cycle information transparently in the background. A real-time monitor observes every single lead processed through the system and collects status changes as sales cycle data points. When a lead is entered into the system, date-stamps mark that lead. Once it is pulled from a partner, worked on, feedback provided, etc., the system marks the data points. Since the process is a real-time process, the data are highly precise. Feedback validation models and other processes support systems make sure that the data are very accurate. In the end, neither the reseller salesperson, nor the lead providing manufacturer needs to enter any data. However, the system develops a management report at the end of each month showing the aggregated sales cycle information across an enterprise and available to drill down to an individual salesperson.

The sales cycle information not only helps the manufacturer to identify training needs within their respective partners but also helps the reseller/owner to identify training needs within his own sales team. In addition to that, even the individual sales people benefit from that information by comparing notes with colleagues on how to shorten sales cycles and improve sales effectiveness.

If your channel is supposed to compete with any direct sales force, a true channel-side sales cycle analysis might be one of the most critical instruments to improve the processes.

Channel Excellence Methodology *suggests that you manage your external sales force as if it were your own team. The partner sales force is in pretty much all aspects identical to an internal sales team.*

3.5. Methodologies for Channel Operations

How to develop Channel Excellence from an operational point of view that is truly embedded in the manufacturer's and partner's business model, business processes and financial model.

3.6.1   Channel Segmentation

3.6.2   Compensation Models

3.6.3   Pricing, Margins and Discounts

3.6.4   Logistics, Product returns and stock protection

3.6.5   Wholesale distribution integration

3.5.1.   Channel Segmentation

This section discusses best practices in segmenting channel partners into groups such as Gold, Silver and Bronze partners or similar classes to reward the very engaged partners with a special status and motivate others to engage more. It also helps structure the discount, compensation and pricing model.

> **Synopsis:** Channel segmentation is a widely used practice and is very well received by the partner community. It helps recognize the very engaged partners. It is a sought after status symbol across all types of partners. It is a good practice is to make the differences very clear and to expose the system to the partner community. It is also a good practice for the manufacturer to refrain from making use of it in front of an end customer. The partner, however, may use it as a competition weapon.

Whether it is a Platinum, Gold and Silver structure, a 5 star system or any other segmentation-using differentiator objects or points, channel segmentation is always very well received by the partner community.

It is important that your partner communication reflects the differences in the status categories. A letter or email stating, "You,, as one of our Platinum Partners, ..." is always a way to reiterate the importance of the partner and the respect you show him. Even, "You, as one of our Bronze Partners are entitled to...." is a nicer and more respectful introduction than just, "You,, as one of our partners,...".

Now, how do you start such a program? Here are a few suggestions:

❖ Your Platinum partners should represent your top 5-10% of your entire partner network – no matter how big or small it is. If the requirements are too high it is not motivating to get there. The only exception is if you just started a channel for the very first time. You may ask for 6-month grace period before you announce platinum partners.

❖ The Gold partners should represent your top 25% of your network. Again, no matter how big or small your channel is.

❖ The Bronze partners should be the top 50%-75% of your channel. A bronze partner however should be only recognized with that title if he either does business with you more than once a year or has another strategic impact to your business such as being an important influencer.

❖

All other partners and the ones who are not very active at all should not be recognized with any status.

One of the next immediate ideas people think of is tying the partner status to revenue. This is by far the most used practice simply because it is so easy to do. However, that does not reflect your strategic intention as a manufacturer. You may have a variety of corporate objectives such as winning market share over your competition. You may need to enter niche markets, or you may want to enter certain customer segments. Partners that are able and willing to help you achieve your corporate objectives should reflect this in their status. A large retail store may earn a lot of revenue and therefore is a Platinum partner, but it does that independent of your strategic directions. It may not be able to help you strategically and simply fulfill demand. This is good and very important to you, but, it will probably do this whether is it a Silver, Gold or Platinum Partner, or even without any status recognition at all. A smaller VAR, however, who has many customers in the health care segment, may be able to get you into this new vertical. It may be of very strategic importance without a lot of revenue. You should consider "paying" it for its engagement with a Platinum Medallion and an associated extra discount.

In any case, the most important part is to very clearly define the rules and make them transparent to *every* partner. Point out exactly what your strategy is, what you are trying to achieve and how the partner levels play into your strategy. Review the rules with your internal team and validate it with a few partners before putting the program into effect. Nothing is more confusing for a partner network than changing a program's rules and goals.

Here are a few examples of how the segmentation may be applied:

1) Simple version

Make a list of all your existing partners, sorted by revenue from the last 12 months.

Take the first 50% of that list and reward them with a status.

Divide the 50% of the partners to whom you apply a status into 3 sections: Top 10%, Top 10-35%, 35-100% for Platinum, Gold and Silver status

Apply the revenue range to those statuses and also apply a discount to each range. Platinum may get 25% discount, Gold may get 22%, Silver may get 20% and all others may get 15% discount.

If the discount range cannot be very big, you may also provide your Platinum Partners with some premium support or extra MDF or Coop marketing funds.

2) Strategic version

Create a list of very important strategic goals. These need to be very precise and descriptive.

Apply the Platinum status to those partners who may actively support your initiatives and work with you based on a clear action plan.

Apply the Gold status to those partners who truly help you to maintain your current status. You may want to enter into a new market but need partners who remain focused on your current bread and butter business. It may be very important to you that you do not lose that basic business while you explore or market into new fields.

Apply the Silver status to the partners who are very interested in your new market and are somewhat engaged but want to wait to see how successful you are. Do not blame them. You may need them as soon as demand is created.

3) Technology version

You may want to create a highly, technically competent channel and request investment on the partner-side for technical expertise.

Create a list of very important training and expertise for which you are looking. Again, those need to be rather precise and descriptive.

Apply the Platinum status to those partners, who are very experienced, have the requested competency and the commitment to engage in the required training.

Apply the Gold status to those partners who are second -tier experts yet very important to your channel strategy. Certain trainings may need to be completed to reach the Gold status.

Apply the Bronze status to those who have the fundamental expertise but still need your experts to execute. Those partners are still important because they at least open doors for you.

Do not run the partner segmentation in a spreadsheet but in a system that is available to your entire channel team. It is a good communication practice, referencing the segmentation whenever you can. Since pricing is attached to most of those programs you need to watch the business rather closely so that the pricing model does not get overwritten too often by special deals. If that happens, in the end the status will become worthless because other rules will overwrite the business practice.

Channel Excellence Methodology suggests that partner segmentation is structured to reflect the strategic objectives of the manufacturer and recognizes the partners with regard to their level of engagement and contribution to reach the corporate objectives. In order to do so, the segmentation needs to be very clear.

3.5.2.   Compensation Issues

This section discusses compensation issues with regard to channel sales and also with respect to channel partners. This section also looks at industry best practices and how compensation may help motivate channel sales people on the manufacturer-side and how it can help prevent channel conflicts.

Synopsis: Compensation and Margin issues are one of the top 4 issues in channels worldwide in all industries. When you understand that your sales people can work on 5 times as many opportunities by working through partners, then they can when they do everything on their own, you figured out that the compensation of your team shall drive exactly that behavior. The compensation for the partner managers need to be in alignment with your corporate goals because those channel managers work with the partners like any other manager with their teams – except that the partners teams are inside partner organizations.

The variety of available compensation models in indirect sales probably hit their peak – I feel there is no more variety than in channels. Some companies provide no extra compensation but just fixed salary, some develop monstrous models to compensate behavior as a mix of partner recruitment, partner satisfaction, revenue, profit, transaction size and program participation – all in one model. Some models are simply revenue through partners, others are based only on profit or a combination of revenue and profit. Some models have kicker for additional business, promotional compensation for additional partners or partners promoting certain new products. All that is still simple compared to the compensation stacks in conjunction with direct sales and channels. So there are models that compensate the direct sales person with commission even if it was sold through partners – just to avoid the channel conflict. As soon as that CFO is fired the company goes back to a "may the best win mentality" and the conflict is defined. Some companies I have seen don't compensate channel sales people because their direct sales force get a simple percentage of revenue regardless where it comes from. The list is endless and I could probably fill a whole book about sales compensation alone.

> **Channels is about getting more business done through partners then you can do on your own.**

In any case this topic is of outmost importance when it comes to a corporate view of the channel. If we take indirect channels as the most economic way of selling products and if we agree that this indirect channel is the backbone of the company's sales force, it is probably easy to decide that the channel sales team need to be compensated based on revenue they do and may be based on the profits they can achieve. If we further understand the indirect channel as a powerful leverage model, we will have no trouble to decide that the leverage only happens if we have our own sales people doing much more business through partners than they could ever do themselves. As the old saying goes "Management is getting things done through other people" nothing is more important than applying this role to channels. "Channels is getting more business done through partners". That said, compensation should be made in the spirit of leverage. First of all a channel sales managers need to have a revenue target that is 3-5 times as high as for an equivalent direct sales person. Otherwise the leverage effect will just not happening. I recently worked with a company where each deal a partner made was completely supported by a channel manager like it would be a direct sales operation. The channel sales person's revenue target was the same then the one from their direct sales force. This was a perfect example of zero leverage and a rightfully ongoing debate about "why do we have a channel?" I have to say I agree – forget your channel and sell direct because the profitability goals can just not achieved that way.

Now, if we agree that a channel manager should have a revenue target of say $3 Million a year, this can only be achieved if the partner manager leverages their channel as best as he can get. This person would have no time to dive deep into projects and hold the partners hand on every step they make. The partner manager needs to be a TRUE MANAGER. He needs to be aware of all the sales going on without being a sales man himself. Only if a sale is at risk, she would step in and help close a deal. Partner managers rightfully earns a compensation that is equivalent to a direct sales manager with the same quota – but with the advantage for the company that there is no expensive team below that person but partners who receive a margin that is slightly lower than the respective direct sales cost would be.

Building a compensation model for channel mangers is probably one of the hardest things to implement because it requires a shift in the company's value thinking. So think LEVERAGE. If the partner manager can't deal with 20-30 high energy channel partners or with 80+ mid size partners or with 200-300 low end partners – something is wrong. The bar is high but that is where the channel not only makes sense but actually develops its power, its financial superiority and its dominance in market penetration. The biggest challenge we all have is that there are not enough highly skilled and successful channel mangers. This in turn is based on the fact that there is not enough education and that is the result of the wide misperception that channels are only for some consumer good products.

Channel Excellence Methodology *suggests that partner managers need to be trained as soon as they start their job and need to be made aware what their responsibility and their reward is. The channel manager should be compensated primarily by revenue with some additional bonus for achieving certain corporate goals like motivating a necessary number of partners to help introduce a new product. Channel sales leaders need to be the biggest revenue contributors in any given company.*

3.5.3. Pricing, Margins & Discounts

This section discusses margin calculation on the manufacturer-side as well as on the channel-side. We will explores who needs what margin and why.

Synopsis: Compensation and Margin issues are one of the top 4 issues in channels worldwide in all industries. DO NOT look at your competitor, but into your books and into your own cost structure! If you can't afford the margin a partner needs to successfully sell, you need to fix it. The margin you provide shall be the same or a bid less what your direct sales force would cost. The reduction in cost of sales with a better return than your direct sales tells you that your channel is the more effective way to sell.

Channel partners are found guilty of getting too creative with their pricing definition, undercutting suggested retail prices and discounting until finally they cannot afford support. Often time's manufacturers define their partner discounts based on what the competition gives, without knowing if there are extra bonuses or compensations or funds provided. Sometimes manufacturers believe that the partner really shouldn't require any margin because they shall make their profits based on their additional services. Margins are the single most argued about topic throughout all channels in all industries. Obviously the partner wants more margins and the manufacturer doesn't want to give away profit. The question is not so much what is the right number but what is the right method.

From a manufacturer point of view it could be rather simple: If the margin the partner gets is 10% less than the manufacturer would pay their direct sales force and the sales force is about 30% of the cost structure, the company would make 3% more profit – in many cases simply DOUBLE their profitability. So the partner margin should not be determined by any of the competitors of that manufacturer but by the company's internal cost structure and ability to control it. A partner margin of 15% tells the world, that this manufacturer is either cheap or has a very efficient way of selling other ways. So a good practice is to understand what the industry average in cost of sale is and guide the partner margin around those numbers.

Even so the relation between margin and sales engagement is so obvious, I have been in so many frustrating answers to the question: "What do you expect the partner do with 15% margin?" – "Don't know that is their business". Well, sorry, it is actually your business and only yours.

It is always a good practice to explore the margin definition together with the companies CFO and a few CEOs on the partner side. Once the CFO understands how the partners run their business and what they can do with the margin they get it is much easier to understand why certain margins may be unnecessary high or too low. Smart manufacturers always try to help the partners running a profitable business – like employers try to make sure their employees are motivated and healthy.

Similarly on the partner side, this discussion could be rather easy. If the manufacturer can't afford to pay a decent margin, it may just be the wrong partner. Also if a manufacturer can't articulate their cost structure and why a certain margin should be enough, I'd be very carefully investing in such manufacturer. But in real life it is not quite as easy as this. Often time's partners invested in manufacturers and through margin erosion and management changes the margin changes to a level the business is just not sustainable any more, at least not the way it has been. Also here, openness is of outmost importance to overcome differences in the margin conversation. A partner, like the manufacturer should be able to articulate why a certain margin is needed or why certain activities just can't be performed any more.

Let's look in an example: A partner organization of 30 people has 12 sales people and a respective 12 people support organization. The partner has 12 manufacturers and sells products into a local market of customers. Let's assume said company does 4.5 Million in revenue and the support organization works profitably contributing $1.5 Million in revenue. Let's further assume the sales people are compensated equally for product and service. At a margin of 10% or $300,000 divided by 12 people, every sales person has a contribution margin of $25,000 per year or $2,000 per month – not enough to feed the team, let alone making a profit. So let's cut the sales team in half to get to $4,000/month, barely enough to pay them. Certainly not enough to do ANY local marketing, let alone new customer acquisition. Now the reduced team works for 4 manufacturers on average – yes, there is leverage. But with 20% margin on average that partner could do a bid more marketing, motivate their team and actually get to profitability.

An additional view in reality is the fact that some of the manufacturers that partner is carrying probably let him do no more than 5% margin because it is a highly competitive market with products that just do no more than 5% margin. The other product lines need to cover that margin loss. Some manufacturers may say: "Forget it I do NOT pay for other manufacturers low margin". OK you don't have to but if you want to have access to that market you have to pay the price. If a Microsoft add-on product shall be sold into the vast Microsoft buyer market – there is a premium to be paid to access this market – nobody can believe this is for free. Manufacturers who hope to get a free ride are typically the ones who loose most. The high tech industry has about 8,000 software companies selling products on an ongoing basis. 7,900 are just not significant simply because they believe that if the customer doesn't take the time to find them and doesn't take the risk to buy their product which is considered the best on the planet the customer doesn't deserve it. 95 of such manufacturers sell through partners, are leveraging the major distributors and reach global markets. And the top 5 of those companies are interestingly enough as big as the other 7,995 and either sell exclusively through the channel like Microsoft, Novell or Symantec or almost exclusively direct such as SAP and Oracle. Even so the later two have channels but those channels are more consultants and technology alliances – not reselling partners.

Could SAP be wildly more successful if they would go entirely through partners? I very much doubt it. My personal opinion is that this would kill SAP like it killed Compaq, just the other way around. Oracle? Oracle is a direct sales culture from top to bottom. And this is a totally fine. The channel is not good for every business and every price range. A $500,000+ solution ala SAP just doesn't make sense to sell through partners. SAP had many attempts to develop a channel and all have failed. I was once part of such a development and realized that a sales team of 7,000 that creates Billions of revenue will overshadow any other sales formation so much that it would die in complete irrelevance. So how could SAP bring a low end product to market? Probably not or only if the company would create a completely separate organization like IBM did in the early 80's when that IBM division even had their own logo color – the "Red IBM". The reintegration of IBM's PC division was the death of that channel and the death of IBM's PCs years and billions in losses later.

So clearly the average price point of the product is an important item to put into the channel mix. It appears to be that the $25,000 mark is an interesting and important price point. Everything above that price point is much harder to sell through channels. Everything above $100,000 almost doesn't make sense to sell through partner channels.

Obviously there are other important aspects in the price and margin calculation. One way to look at it is how you compete. But remember aligning the margin with your competitors is not getting you anywhere unless it is coincidently the same margin. But if you want to attract partners you may pull extra margin out of your market8ing budget or out of your profitability – but clearly you NEED TO KNOW what effect a change in margin has to your cost structure and profitability. If a product sells like crazy and the only reason to have a channel is the ability to have local product availability, a lesser margin may be acceptable. In those cases the high demand often is generated by well done marketing initiatives. The partners have less or no work to sell it and therefore may be fine with 10% margin.

But the more likely scenario is that the channel need to create local awareness, attract local customers and actively sell the product into its installed base. This cost sales resources and requires initiatives that need to be financed somehow. 20% margin is probably needed and more is often required. Sometimes it is very hard to introduce new products and so the margin need to be even further increased to convince partners to invest into local initiatives. But this is another very important dynamic to understand: Partners are willing and able to INVEST. Probably in sum more than even big manufacturers can afford. At Infinigate we had 4,000 partners in the Internet high days. When we announced brand new products, and offered an initial margin of 40% for the first 6 month, our partners were very engaged and started local initiatives. At least half of our partners got engaged and invested in those new products – and if it was just about $1,000 on average. Times 2,000 partners, that was $2,000,000 right there – we would never be able to do that on our own.

I remember one day I met with Jost Stollman in a Pizzeria in Cologne Germany. Jost just quit his job Bain & Company and told me he is going to build the largest reseller organization in Europe. He explained me his concept and he said he will need the best margin and some extra points on top. In turn he will buy everything from us (Computer 2000). An hour later we had the deal. I simply trusted that he could do it. A year later he was one of the top 10 customers and 2 years later he was our largest reseller. 5 years later he was the largest European reseller and CompuNet was bought by General Electric. There was a huge risk: He could take the extra margin and win based on a better purchase price. Instead he kept his promise and built the most successful high profile sales force of all channel partners in Europe.

So the margin conversation not only shouldn't be seen as a thread and something we try to avoid, not it is strategically of outmost importance to fully understand any aspect of it and navigate our company with that knowledge.

Channel Excellence Methodology suggests that the pricing for partners are ideally products below the $10,000 mark (not necessarily deal size but product price .The margin the partners can operate on should be in the 20% range and above if the partner is expected to actively sell and market the product in their respective market. If the product sells on its own, the margin may be less and if it is very hard to sell the respective product or is up against very dominant competitors, the margin may need to go up as high as 40-50%.

3.5.4. Logistics, Product Returns and Stock Protection

Discussing the role of logistics between partner and manufacturer, best practices in returns and stock or warehouse protection methods. Not only is this important in the partner relationship but connects deep into each company's reporting practice and compliance.

Synopsis: The product and service flow between partners and producers has to be as accurate and well documented as if the product would have been sold to an end customer. On the services side it is important to understand revenue recognition and help partners to become part of the reporting cycle. Moving the responsibility to sell products to the partner by pumping up their warehouses is one of the worst practices in partner relationships.

In the old days of the high tech boom it was an often seen practice that manufacturers simply pumped products into the warehouses of distributors and larger resellers to show good quarter end results. Today this is actually illegal – at least for public companies because the company betrays their investors with incorrect revenue numbers. But whether legal or not - it is certainly not a good practice. Still today you will find large stores with millions worth of excess inventory because they bought the product and can't return them. Deals are closed where the buyer (partner) agrees to a certain price but commits not to return any of those goods. Companies like Overstock became in existence that then buy those unsellable products and find new markets and attractive enough prices to actually sell those products. The product flow from a producer to market often times goes over multiple channels before they eventually land at a customer. The pricing mix a channel partner can entertain is complex and often times one of their best kept secrets. The manufacturer in turn has to be open to those deals in order to participate in markets they just couldn't participate otherwise.

Now those strangely sold products once in a while return. Sometimes from the partner they were sold to sometimes not. Product returns can become a real difficult and sometimes a legal issue. Manufacturers are requested to put very clear and legally as well as customer friendly return policies in place.

One of the good practices is definitely that a product may be retuned any time at no penalty as long as it was not used and can be resold. Of products flow through multiple tiers such as distributors to master resellers and then to local resellers, the vender is better off to define the return policies BEFORE the first products may come back. If a sales person in the channel only caught a fain of a thought that product returns are difficult, he or she would no longer recommend that manufacturer and the manufacturer may never find out what the broken link was.

Ever returned a product and were asked to pay 10% "restocking" fee? Did you ever buy a product their again? May be but only if you were 100% certain you keep it – right? I would never buy any product from Best Buy unless I'm very certain I keep it. If I am not 100% sure I go somewhere else. Not that I buy products with the intention to return it but I may decide otherwise later on. This convenience is one reason why consume is so much higher in the US compared to Europe. In most European countries you can't return products at all. Therefore less is consumed and the economy is less lively. As a manufacturer you need to fully understand that dynamic on order to make your partners successful.

At Computer 2000, today TechData and later at Infinigate we would not accept a manufacturer without stock protection and stock rotation policy. A channel just can't take the risk of "none movers", products that don't move in the warehouse.

Good practice in "Stock Rotation" is to allow a partner to return any "none movers" within no more than 90 days after purchase against a new purchase order. In other words if the partner does not sell a product within 90 days he has the right to return it and order new products worth the product value he returned. If he keeps the product longer and fails to return it he can't return it later on. Another good practice is to provide "Stock Price Protection". So if the partner purchased a product for let's say $500 and the manufacturer introduces a price decrease to $450, the partner will get a reimbursement of $50 per product that the partner still has on stock.

In order to accurately police the two above mentioned programs it is essential to have constantly up to date reports of the partner's warehouse situation. This for instance is one of the major reasons manufacturers having distributors to manage their logistics. However not all distributors have a well managed mechanism in place to track their partners inventories. So distributors may accept returns but can't return to manufacturers if the returns are out of date. Or manufacturers do not honor the distributor accepting returns from their resellers. In either case it is important to know those edge cases and define it either way.

Another related topic is revenue recognition, especially as Software as a Service is becoming main stream. With SaaS partners no longer "resell" any physical goods but virtual software services. The rise of the SaaS industry will unfold one of the biggest partnership opportunities in High Tech history. Logistic is essentially zero, no product to move, no returns, no logistic. The logistic is really the providing of the service on an ongoing basis. Manufacturers are requested to provide the software service on an ongoing basis with 99.xx % availability. And that is exactly the point that needs to be understood from a financial and liability point of view. The manufacturer and as part of the sales chain also the partner can only recognize the service that has been delivered in a given month. Logistic has so to say virtualized. Accounting principles say that only the service that has been delivered can be recognized as revenue – hence the term "Revenue Recognition". Even if the customer pays for one year up front, the recognizable revenue is only for the service that was delivered by that time. In other words, if a customer decided to buy Software as a Service for $100 per month and pays for the first year $1,200 the time he signs the contract. That very day actually the revenue is zero. After the 6th month the recognizable revenue is $600, after 9 month $900 and when the year is over and the service is completed the $1,200 can be recognized as revenue. This short explanation shall not serve as an explanation of revenue recognition, it barely scratches the surface – but as channel manager on either side you need to understand the existence.

Channel Excellence Methodology suggests that you clearly and generously define your logistic, product return and reporting practice. Protect the partners investment in stocking your products by offering full price protection for at least 30 days and full stock rotation for 90 days. Request a weekly stock report and help your partners to optimize their warehouse. The more optimized a partners logistic is the better is your own logistic and product planning. Train your partners in the way you recognize revenue.

3.5.5. Whole Sale Distribution Integration

Discussing the role of a "true" distributor in a multi tier channel organization and how and when to engage with distribution partners.

Synopsis: Distributors are very large intermediary logistics and sales organizations with great buying power and a huge, often global network of resellers, dealer and other channel partners. Distributors are often misunderstood as manufacturers hope that distributors are marketing engines or resellers hope that distributors provide comprehensive technical support. The role of an international distributor often varies a great deal from national distributors. Also more and more Value Added Distributors come into the scene and provide typically very different kind of services.

It is important to understand the 3 very different types of distributors:

1) National Distributor, a distributor servicing resellers in the same nation the manufacturer is headquartered. Typically provides the volume logistics and financial services, to help a manufacturer reach out to thousands of smaller specialized national resellers.

2) International Distributor, a distributor servicing foreign resellers where the manufacturer may have a sales office but

is not headquartered. Typically provides volume logistics and financial services, to help manufacturers reach out to resellers in dispersed foreign countries. Those distributors typically also manage to be the proxy between manufacturer and national customers and all kinds of partners to which the manufacturer has no access otherwise.

3) Value Added Distributors, typically an international distributor who provides additional distribution services and has a very different internal structure relative to the larger volume distributors. Typically provides partner recruitment and development services, initial training and support services as well as some marketing services and represents also some smaller manufacturers. Some of the value added functionality may contain project support for more complex products.

This chapter is kind of a natural for me since I founded the largest European Distributor Computer 2000 and later the largest European Internet Products Distributor Infinigate. While Computer 2000 was a prototype of an International Volume Distributor, Infinigate was one of the first Value Added Distributors. Even so both types of companies look pretty similar from the outside, there are some major differences:

The heart of a volume distribution organization is its highly perfected logistics and financial transaction mechanism. Such a distributor is able to receive, store, ship and even return products faster and cheaper than even the largest manufacturer. That's why companies including IBM, Microsoft, HP, Cisco and many others choose to simply ship all their products to a few distributors and let them distribute the products to literally hundred thousands of resellers around the world. In order to achieve such a high degree of efficiency, every possible step in the sales chain need to be optimized to the Nth degree. There is no room for error and no room for experiments. Manufacturers, Distributors and Resellers need to be a well collaborating team in order to deliver pretty much everything to anybody within a day. Millions of goods are not only shipped but invoiced, credited, thousands get returned and a distributor needs to built this massive logistics engine in order to compete. Products need to be in high demand and that way a volume distributor is able to process the goods for a few percentage points of margin. This is why volume distributors require typically minimum revenue of $10 Million per year per manufacturer. The sweet spot of a volume distributor is a $50 Million revenue manufacturer. Large volume distributors are well above the $1Billion level of annual revenue.

But what happens to smaller manufacturers, new technologies, new market segments, where there is no high demand, partners need to be initially recruited and products require consultative selling?

This is where the VAD (Value Added Distributor) comes into play. In contrast to a volume distributor, a VAD has a very different internal structure. There are not thousands of products of the same kind to be delivered daily. There are no hundreds of financially risky resellers. There is no high demand that just need to be fulfilled. There are very different challenges to be dealt with. A VAD for instance helps smaller manufacturers who just started to sell internationally to reach out to broader markets where the VAD helps with partner recruitment programs. Often times the manufacturer has not the funds to establish a complete international office with all the sales, marketing, service and support services. Instead the manufacturer may simply sponsor a person within the VAD who is then working exclusively for this manufacturer but leverages all the facilities, the team and services of the value added distributor. A VAD has an internal structure for customized marketing initiatives and is able to handle the projected demand without requiring full load of their logistics engine. A VAD provides typically other services like product training for the resellers and even joins the reseller's sales teams in larger projects. Of course those services are not for free. A VAD requires a much higher margin structure than a volume distributor – otherwise he cannot provide those services. A VAD is easily able to handle product lines below $1 Million per year. The revenue sweet spot is probably around $5 – 10 Million per year per manufacturer. VADs range between $50 to $500 Million in revenue.

When is a good time to engage a distributor? First and foremost if there is at least some demand for the product that a manufacturer has a hard time to support with his own team. Neither the volume distributor nor the VAD can create demand. Hoping that the distributor with all their resellers can create demand and ramp up the manufacturer's revenue is probably one of the most common misunderstanding in the distribution chain. Demand can only be created at the end user or end consumer level – a distributor has no structure to actually create demand with end consumers. However a VAD is at least able to act as an intermediary between manufacturer and reseller to stimulate the reseller to introduce a product to their installed base. But as resellers are very careful with their customer base, don't expect a big marketing push – this as stated earlier in this book is and remains one of the most important responsibilities of the manufacturer himself.

3.5.6.   Channel Types and Product Life Cycle

This section discusses the various types of channels as well as the respective sales channel requirements from a product life cycle point of view.

> **Synopsis**: Different products and different target markets require different types of channels. It is important to determine not only what type of channel you need to address your target audience, but also what type of channel you need relative to the product life cycle stage. New technologies may need different types of channels compared to the same product 5 years later when the product is matured, the technology well-adopted in the market and service requirements have changed.

There might be many more channel types, but in order to avoid too many details, we will discuss the following four groups:

- Resellers (Dealers, Agents)

- Value Added Resellers (VARs)

- Catalysts (SaaS Channel)

- Distributors

Each group has its very specific value to market and sell into a given target audience. One important aspect to keep in mind is that your product is moving within a product life cycle that most likely will change the type of channel you need over time.

Rather than deciding only what channel you will need today you should keep in mind what channel you will need as the product matures or actually moves into pure maintenance mode. In the chapter on partner profiling we discussed some of those details.

If we take the product category *firewall* for instance, a product that protects a company network from intruders, we know that in the early 90's those products were implemented only by specialized VARs and security experts. In order to sell a firewall through partners, a manufacturer had to know and understand those VARs. Today, small businesses buy their firewall from CDW and run an automatic install. However, larger companies with increased security requirements may need not only a VAR for implementation, but also a security consultant. The market has obviously changed; it is now much bigger and shows a very diverse requirements profile. As products and markets change, so does the channel change. Sometimes the partners themselves change; sometimes new or other partners need to be recruited.

It is a good practice to review the current channel relative to product development, market trends and changes in customer behavior. Similarly, it is a good practice for channel partners to review their manufacturer profiles relative to their customer and market development.

3.5.7.   Going from local to global

This section was contributed by Harald Horgen, CEO The York Group, one of the thought leaders and channel masterminds. It discusses some key thoughts moving from a local channel to global indirect business.

Synopsis: Cultural differences are overestimated and underestimated at the same time. Going global obviously needs planning but the most important suggestion we are giving here is go there, talk to other vendors, partners and distributors AND customers to get a feel for yourself. Don't make a big push but a few carefully planned steps and build your channel based on your very own experience. And take care of the obvious: localized products and a well defined support infrastructure.

I have seen literally hundreds of companies fail when going International. It happens with an unbelievable precise pattern of mistakes. It is easy to produce a simple list with dos and don'ts. Obviously there may be other mistakes involved but here are the key topics you should carefully consider:

Product localization:

I hate to generalize too much but whatever you sell internationally, make sure it is translated and localized. Note the difference: translation means manuals and the product appearance itself, in particular software. Localized means you product or service is aware of international date and time format, different address formats, different local electrical or mechanical requirements and laws and sometimes even taste and appearance may be something to consider.

Local Office

Think you need to setup a local office to support the foreign market? Wrong. International markets in all industries are used to buy international products from all industries. So I feel it is more important to build local alliances and leverage the dynamic a new foreign product can create and support those local partners rather than building an office that need to establish and still most of the time is rather local to where ever the office starts. Certainly at some point in time in the years to come it will make sense but typically it is more important to create success with local partners who are very familiar with foreign manufacturers than start with a local office. But there is 1 exception. If you are a car producer and want to have success, you need to have a German office and manufacturing line in order to be even considered. Or if you are a French Software Manufacturer and want to play in the US market, you need to have a US office with US engineers and a US product and no referral to a French headquarter.

Product Support

Of course you need to support your product locally – train your partners. In all industries there is a set of partners who are very successful with foreign products. Pick those and train them and pay them – save the money you would put in a local support team until the volume is there and your international revenue is over 10% of your local revenue.

Partner Selection

Make absolutely sure you know who you are signing up and set very clear expectations. Likewise you need to make sure that also you can deliver on the expectation you set about yourself. Language and cultural differences do an overwhelming job to mislead anyway – so make sure you can articulate and understand what the expectations on both sides are. The influential network of partners is often times much underestimated or even unknown. Xeequa has recently established a large list of high tech partners around the world. This may be an additional source to check.

Pricing

Increase the price internationally a bid to make up for the additional cost. Wrong! So often seen so less understood. Thanks to the Internet everybody knows every price. Trust me on that one of you don't think so. A different price would do 2 things: 1) open up grey imports. 2) Negative impression to the partner and consumer because you would obviously try to take advantage of the international difference. You may have 100 arguments why, people won't listen but be disappointed. Grey imports

In the synopsis of this chapter I mentioned that people overestimate and underestimate international business at the same time. Here is what I mean: You will hear the sentence "Here in XYZ Land business is conducted very different than ion your country" in every single conversation you have. (unless the other person read this book). After 25 years of international business in 5 continents I can say – business is conducted pretty much the same around the world. It's buy and sell and the contracts to engage with partners vary only marginally between Germany, Singapore, Australia, Kuweit or India. The constantly growing globalization and the interest to make it easy has come to a point that the technical way of conducting business is pretty much the same. Differences in basic business mechanics are often completely overestimated. On the other hand, social interaction still varies dramatically and this is what many completely underestimate. Business is done between people. Business is done with people. And cultures change much slower. The development of virtualization in the US is way ahead of Europe. People rather meet than do a quick web conference. Geographic differences are something else you need to take in account. While in France most of the business is done in Paris, the Parisian are not too welcome outside Paris, find an additional location. Germany, similar in size than France has not that metropolitan structure around a major city but at least 5 major areas including Berlin, Frankfurt, Munich, Duesseldorf and Hamburg. In the UL you have London but a rather interesting market in the northern UK. Similar in India, in particular since the rise of the technology sector, there are at least 3 areas to cover.

One of the most experienced consultant in international channels, in particular Europe International that I know of is Harald Horgen, CEO of The York Group. When I talked to him recently he provided me with some very good insight that I just want to reproduce here:

International markets are littered with vendors who went overseas on the strength of their product – "we are the only company that does ..." The truth is that the technology plays a very small part in the success of a company. Yes, the product needs to be good, it needs to have a clear market opportunity, and it needs to be well-supported. But success in going from local to global will be based much more on the quality of the relationship that is established with the new partners. If there is no buy-in from the resellers, if they do not invest in a focused sales and marketing program, it doesn't really matter how good the product is.

Resellers and distributors in foreign markets are used to being disappointed by their vendors, and in some cases being deceived and abused. How many times do channel partners find themselves building a market for a new vendor, only to be displaced after a few years because the vendor either sets up a direct sales operation or is acquired by a larger company that has its own sales and distribution network in the target market? As a result, resellers will often see a new vendor as a risk as much as an opportunity, and they will take a very close look at them before deciding to invest their time, money and people resources in building the market for them.

In going from local to global, profitability becomes a function of distance and trust. In other words, the further away a vendor is from its partners, the more critical the level of trust becomes, and this is particularly true during the first 3-6 months of a relationship. Once a relationship has been in place for several years the occasional lapse or hiccup will be accepted, but this is not the case in the months after the contract has been signed. Having been burned in the past, resellers will be looking for red flags; they will be looking for an excuse not to invest in the new product.

For a vendor starting to expand overseas this means that they have to do everything possible to gain the reseller's trust. This starts during the recruitment process, from the time the first contact is made. The reseller will be evaluating the vendor on their initial approach (was this an opportunistic call, or part of a structured channel recruitment program?); the channel strategy (will the vendor be protecting its partners with a careful market segmentation strategy, or signing as many resellers as they can find?); the quality of the channel program (can they count on the vendor to provide the right training and on-going support?); and marketing support (is the partner expected to do everything on its own, or does the vendor have a co-marketing program). A vendor can't recruit good partners without being a good partner.

Channel Excellence Methodology suggests that you plan a trip to the key areas and talk to distributors, partners and customers. IN Europe, visit the UK, France and Germany and because Italy so beautiful visit people in Milano or Roma. Make sure you meet with good representation of your target group – most importantly potential customers. Have a partner manager who is responsible exclusively for International.

3.6. How to transform a company from direct to indirect?

This section discusses the challenges to turn a direct sales organization into a channel sales organization.

> **Synopsis**: To change from direct sales to indirect sales is probably one of the most difficult changes in the life of a company. And as this is very different from company to company, there is no cookbook like approach. I highly recommend engaging a very qualified consulting firm to guide the executive team through the process.

First and foremost this is a strategic decision that needs to be made with exceptional care. The decision needs to be made nowhere else than on the top: The CEO and his executive team in conjunction with his board. Once that decision is made the company needs to create a transformation plan that includes a career path for the sales team as the most critical component.

Become a manager
Become a manager and guide for the channel. Instead of hunting himself/herself, the new channel sales manager needs to become a true manager and mentor and help the channel partners to sell every single opportunity that is out there. There is no such thing like an "experienced" channel sales person. The better the support and the more collaboration with the manufacturer is offered, the faster the partner can close. Furthermore, the more partners sign up, the more robust the support plan and the busier the

manufacturer sales people get. It is all about management – getting things done through others.

Join the partner
Join the partners sales team as a leader and experienced hunter. If well designed, this could be extremely successful for all parties. The sales person usually will become a more important at the partner organization, often even joining the partners' management team. Also with all the experience that sales person brings he/ she may be even more successful in the new environment. The Reseller at the same time gets a highly trained new employee who should be able to produce instant success.

Of course there is a risk that a sales person is not interested in either position and leaves – even to the competition. These complications will bother the company's management team and other employees for a while, maybe even a year. After that the company will be known for its very clear strategy, its very clear management style and its transparent execution. Pretty much every company in the high tech space needed to start with a direct sales model.

Interesting enough the most successful companies chose a very clear and exclusive sales strategy after all. Companies like Cisco, Microsoft, Symantec, Novell, Compaq (in the old days), Dell and several others sell exclusively direct or indirect. Each company went through a difficult but very successful transition and returned much stronger to the market.

I happened to have many conversations in the early days with Microsoft executives at a time when Microsoft had still a mix of direct and indirect sales. Christian Wedell, later President of Microsoft Europe explained me why they still have some direct accounts and what their plans are to move it from direct to indirect. He urged me to trust that the company has a long term vision about channels and we have to help overcome this critical phase of conversion. He was so clear about every step they are doing so that I bought into it and in turn made our partners aware of the Microsoft strategy. At the time I already had to convince over 1,000 partners to buy in. The rest is history. Microsoft turned a loose sales model in the course of 2 years to a channel only model.

Very large players such as IBM, HP failed to make those decisions and despite their size wasn't very successful in the various fields they tried to reach. It was never because of their products but because of the high cost, redundancy and friction in their sales operation. Of course IBM and HP are very successful companies. But they could not outperform their competitors despite their size. IBM needed to sell their PC division to Lenovo after billions of dollars of losses and HP makes money with all sorts of products but not with their computers.

A transformation to an exclusive direct or exclusive indirect model would help even those very large companies to refocus and win back market share. But instead of focusing on the power partner networks, they let other players such as Acer becoming very strong and may be a new leader in that field.

4. Creating a new SaaS Catalyst Business

The new Software as a Service Industry needs to develop a whole new category of partnership. This chapter describes ways for a partner company to participate and succeed in the services-driven economy.

4.1   Introduction

4.2   Definition of a SaaS Catalyst

4.3   Creating a Catalyst

4.1. Introduction

While this chapter discusses the differences of a Software as a Service channel relative to the standard software channels it is a representative for variations in channels in general. It is interesting to learn however that the basic mechanisms of channel s as reselling units of producing companies are the same, yet there are big differences to understand. One of the key differences to understand with this example is the difference in reselling services versus products.

4.2. Definition of a SaaS Catalyst

A SaaS Catalyst is defined as a company or even individual that helps users or customers to select the best possible SaaS application for their company or use case and with that helps the SaaS industry to get broader awareness. A SaaS Catalyst does not produce SaaS Software themselves but helps customers to implement such systems, help customers to adjust business processes or align business processes with the new software. Typically there is no technical expertise needed at all other then configuring a software for it's business case in a browser.

Unlike traditional VARs, who typically have a lot of technology expertise, SaaS Catalysts have a lot business process expertise.

4.3. Creating a Catalyst

This section discusses how one could create a new catalyst and participate in the SaaS industry.

> **Synopsis**: Building a catalyst is, in general, no different than starting any other high tech business. However, the way catalysts work is different compared to the traditional VAR or reseller. The differences are mostly in the way a customer expects to be serviced. A manufacturer delivers their solution, but the service profile is no longer technology driven but instead requires a good understanding of industry-specific business processes.

The SaaS industry is new. The way SaaS manufacturers do their business is new, and so is the channel in this new world. Catalysts, the new breed of business partners in the SaaS industry are also creating a whole new way of servicing the manufacturers products and helping customers be more successful.

Two very important channel thought leaders are Marc Benioff from Salesforce.com and Subrah Ayar from Webex, now part of Cisco. Mark developed a channel early on knowing that at the end of the day CRM is just a product but the Internet holds more than that. He also understood that channels will extend an expensive direct sales force in many aspects. And while the early attempts to build a channel were not overly successful, Salesforce.com had the time to learn. AppExchange is a very successful platform and the channel is represented by close to 1,000 partners building products and therefore pushing salesforce.com as a platform to be able to sell their products. The salesforce.com channel today is very different than the general IT channel. Salesforce.com partners are primarily developers, similar to Microsoft in the early days. We will see a dramatic shift from the developer community to a reselling community in the next few years. I had many conversations with Lonnie Wills, a VP of worldwide services at Astadia, the largest Salesforce.com implementer. Astadia is a true Value Added Reseller to Salesforce.com. More of those will be needed to grow the market. While Salesforce.com has a clear market leadership position in the SaaS based CRM space with over 30,000 customers, we need to know that there are over 8 Million registered businesses in the US that have customers and will sooner or later use a computer based system to better track their customers. On a worldwide scale we have an estimated 30 Million businesses who deal with more than 50 customers and will at one point in time use a customer management system. That means that Salesforce.com has only 0.1% market share. It will take tens of thousands of implementers to saturate the market.

A slightly different approach was taken by Webex. I had the opportunity to talk with Subrah Ayar many times and was impressed by his vision to leverage channels to grow a worldwide business. Interestingly enough Webex doesn't have any channel to speak of but a very effective direct sales force, probably one of the best in the world. So why not channels despite the vision? Well, the market is still very early on. Webex is just now creating the Webex Connect platform that will engage partners to build application but more importantly a platform to sell applications. While Salesforce.com is focusing on products that provide added functionality to Salesforce.com Webex Connect is build to sell any SaaS application. And given the early stage of the market, it will be interesting to see which or whether both models will succeed in the long term.

4.4. Top Ten Aspects for Building a Successful Catalyst Business

(1) Customers – As a new catalyst, your customer base will most likely be smaller teams or individuals in business organizations moving from onsite servers and software to an on-demand model. Those customers no longer want to deal with technology. They just want to get their job done whether it is sales, marketing, administration, HR, logistics, production, service.... You will find these people in home office-based companies all the way up to global enterprises. The old SOHO – SMB – Enterprise categorization is out of synch when we talk SaaS. We are talking about "consuming services" and that happens equally in small and large corporations. The big difference is that IT is still involved in large corporations.

(2) Manufacturers – There are over 300 manufacturers today, with many looking for partners to help sell, market, implement, integrate and service their solutions. While it was hard to build a business around 1 or 2 SaaS solutions, today you will find pretty much every application as SaaS model.

Building a portfolio is much easier, but not all manufacturers understand how to deal with partnerships.

(3) Services – SaaS catalysts will not resell any products. Instead they will create a portfolio of value added services, many of which cannot be provided by the manufacturers but are required by the customers. Here are some examples:

▶ *Deployment service* – Help organizations or teams deploy a solution by creating some internal standards, methods of operations, and rules of engagement and designing workflow processes for that team. This may be ways of jointly using CRM, campaign management, HR systems or others. Even so, SaaS applications are easy to use, once multiple people use the same application.

▶ *Configuration Service* – SaaS applications are highly flexible and configurable in order to meet the needs of all customers. The flexibility comes with the need to configure a system to the customer's profile. This may not be very complicated but takes time and requires a thoughtful and organized approach for a few days. As companies change their organizations and software grows in features, configurations are no longer static, but become an ongoing activity. Catalysts need to be able to service the customer on an ongoing basis. Here comes the concept of the "Recurring Services Model".

▶ *Integration* – Integrating one SaaS application with another is one of those engagements where typically neither manufacturer gets engaged, but an independent third party, like a catalyst, can perform the task. If the integration needs to be done on the premises, software catalysts will usually outperform any manufacturer. As software changes, integrations need to be kept alive. Integration will therefore have a one time and a recurring revenue component for the catalyst.

≫ *Business Process Alignment* – As SaaS applications are technically very simple; customers have more time and availability to optimize the actual use of the software. Catalysts have the opportunity to provide coaching and consulting support to their customers by working with them to optimize their business processes and align process and application for better workflow, more effective reporting and growing business effectiveness. With simpler tools and a shorter attention span from customers, those services will no longer be purchased from expensive global consulting firms but from business savvy and application experienced catalysts.

≫ *Reporting & Analytics Services* – Catalysts create a whole new service when they begin to help their customers interpret their business results and compare them with other available industry data. As Meta data are more and more public, aggregated by many SaaS companies, customers will want to engage in benchmark comparisons and to better understand their potential to improve. While those services were extremely expensive and often times impossible to get in the traditional software world, SaaS opens up a whole new service category.

≫ *Training and Support* – The obvious real quick: Training people on the new SaaS application is no different than on other software. However, because SaaS applications compete by being easy to use, training is less lengthy but more individual, based on the individual configuration; likewise with support. Since the application is run by the provider, there is no tech support to be given, no system configuration, update, etc. However, there is a need for supporting the business-related use of the application on an ongoing basis.

(4) Target Market – While traditionally in the IT world a VAR would focus their business geographically and sell locally to all kinds of businesses, a SaaS catalyst would need to focus their business by vertical industries to be able to better help a customer with business process issues and alignment processes with available applications. At least in the next few years, customers will prefer a business savvy catalyst from another city over a local provider with less business expertise.

(5) Portfolio – It is easy to create a whole portfolio of applications and services around a specific vertical today. Adjacent solutions may round up a solution portfolio. It would make sense, for instance, if you are providing HR solutions as a core application also offering recruiting solutions, social network solutions, career building solutions, training solutions and even web conferencing solutions to perform the respective trainings over distances. This should be bundled with the respective services, implementation, configuration, data maintenance, report review and quarterly performance analysis. The same would work in sales, marketing, operations, etc.

(6) Business Model – Unlike in the traditional IT industry, there is no big product margin. The catalyst's business model however is more autonomous and less dependent on the health of the respective application manufacturer. Customers will pay for the various services typically in an ongoing, recurring revenue stream. Those services together with the SaaS license fees are still less expensive compared with traditional software and the entire IT overhead. Therefore, catalysts will make money by providing the services, receiving some referral fees from manufacturers for new business they have acquired as well as a percentage of the recurring SaaS revenue. As catalysts begin helping customers assemble whole application sets, manufacturers will appreciate the catalyst considering their solutions.

(7) Competition The early competition, like in any emerging industry, will come from those manufacturers who do not understand channels and fight for every business directly. However, there is no industry where direct business supersedes indirect, partnership-based business models. Like any other industry, there is only so much room for direct sellers; the majority is partner-based as the surviving model. Over time, new competing catalysts will enter the market and compete with the more established group. Most likely, competition will be fought over expertise and completeness of a service portfolio.

(8) Profile – A catalyst profile is ideally a startup company or a very independent group within an existing consulting firm. The consultants within a catalyst are customer service-oriented and business-savvy consultants with a deep understanding of the respective SaaS applications. Unlike manufacturer-independent consultants who want to keep their independence and do not want to be associated with any brand – catalysts in contrast are associated with specific brands and have a deep understanding of those products, how to configure, implement and manage those applications. The catalysts work closely with manufacturers and their product teams to be up-to-date and act as knowledge transformers to the customers. I can easily see young MBA students after just a few years business practice starting their own catalyst business.

(9) Sales and Marketing – Catalysts are like any business always looking for new customers. A catalyst will find those customers by working closely with application manufacturers, advertising their service on the internet, being present at events and most importantly by word of mouth. Other ways of identifying new opportunities are by reading Internet Forums where people are looking for help and exposing their pain points. Industry associations like the SIIA or platforms like Tanooma are other places to find additional business opportunities. In order to quickly ramp up awareness and customer success, a catalyst will need to ensure satisfied customers and build a portfolio of solutions fast. **(10) Financial Model** – Catalysts will be small startups or small groups within consulting firms that have a low-cost structure afforded by the early users in the industry. With no costly overhead, catalysts will win customers fast because their services are affordable and lead to faster results than internal resources. Hence, new catalyst firms will financially outperform established consulting firms and at the same time have a better understanding of customer needs by focusing on the SaaS model. There is no capital expenditure requirement to build a SaaS catalyst other than operational startup cost for an office environment and finding the first customers.

5. Systems Supporting the Methodologies

This chapter discusses tools that help manufacturers and partners to better collaborate. The role Portals and PRM systems play and how next generation Alliance Collaboration Systems work

5.1   Partner Portals

5.2   PRM systems

5.3   Alliance Collaboration Systems

5.1.Partner Portals

This section explores the needs of partner portals and how to build a successful portal system.

> **Synopsis**: Partner portals have a different meaning to the manufacturer than to the partners. The portal design needs to be around the partner's needs and their expectations not a branding tool for the manufacturer.

When you talk to manufacturers you will often hear that they are busy improving the partner portal by putting more information up and hoping that generates more "traffic." The success of a partner portal is measured by the traffic it generates. How about measuring the partner portal by level of partner satisfaction? Also here people often are mistaking "quality for quantity."

I talked to the partner community and they provided me with a nice repertoire of things they wanted in a portal. The list is in the order of priorities. Number 1 should catch all our attention:

- Structure, ease of navigation and indexing

- Processes: What are the processes for support, warranty issues, returns, and other requests?

- Contacts: Who do I contact in what kind of situation?

- Value proposition for each product you sell

- Competitive advantage – and who are those competitors

- Case studies and reference customers

- Company overall strategy

- Easy to read price list

- Partner program information about lead distribution, deal registration, MDF funds management etc.

- Technical documentation for everything you sell

- Marketing material and images for download

- News, events and all the rest

Now, when I asked the manufacturer community and I was luck to match some of those topics the order is exactly reverse. Manufacturers start with the News first and with structure last.

As partners will use many manufacturer portals, do not expect anybody "lives" in your portal, let the partner get in quickly, find exactly what they need, get out and sell! When building a portal you may go through the following simple checklist:

1) Sort the requests from your partners based on priority and start from the top. Keep in mind: it is THEIR TOOL at first, and only second a branding instrument for your company. Build an easy to understand structure and easy to use information pages.

2) Make it easy to access the portal for ALL members in your channel. Do not kill yourself with complicated security rules to access the content

3) Think of the portal traffic as a representation of the agility of your channel in general – not so much the attractiveness of your portal. If your channel is not very active – the best portal in the world would not show traffic.

In the last 5 years I followed many discussions in regards to partner portal and PRM systems. The ideal partner portal is also a PRM system or the ideal PRM system contains a partner portal.

However, the ideal combination never really exists. Either a partner portal has some custom built attached PRM-like features or a PRM system offers some rudimentary, but not satisfying, portal features. I learned that the conflict is based on the fundamentally different approach each system has.

While a PRM system is a productized piece of software that is simply configured to the manufacturers needs like one configures any other software – even the buttons of your spreadsheet, but the general look and feel is still a standard product. In contrast a partner portal has a strong branding component and is supposed to deliver the partner information in a branded way as well. Standardized process-based software and custom branded portal simply do not go very well with each other. As a result, we typically see custom portals branded to the manufacturers flavor, and those portals provide access to PRM or PRM-like applications.

5.2. PRM Systems

This section discusses the state of the PRM systems market and how and when PRM systems help channel managers.

Synopsis: PRM (Partner Relationship Management) systems were the early answer to the need to better and systematically manage business partners. PRM systems provide partner database functionality and a set of partner-related tools such as lead distribution, and partner program management.

After the first success wave of CRM people got the idea of better customer relationships and tried to apply the same concept to the channel. So they called it PRM (Partner Relationship Management). However, they soon understood that it is not so much the relationship to the partner that needs to be managed. More importantly it was the business processes and initiatives from the manufacturer that needed better management. Early PRM systems were not a great success. Many software companies just added a PRM Module to their particular suites. Once integrated into ERP, CRM or Financial packages, PRM at least provided a bit more value to better track the partner and their revenue data, marketing allowances or service requests. However, PRM still did not help in the most important aspect of the relationship: *selling*. With CRM, the selling is done by a salesperson, who knows the customer in great detail. An enterprising salesperson, using a well-deployed CRM system knows the customer's buying behavior, the responsibilities of all the players in its customer's enterprise, and understands the support requirements. Furthermore, he can manage the contracts and proposals and can track all sorts of customer-specific initiatives, customizing projects and so forth. But once you use a channel, all those features are of less importance. Channel partners mostly serve the mid-market and requirements are very different. Managing the partners in a database is certainly somewhat important but, again, *it does not help sell.*

PRM systems are typically a one-way street and are usually just used and facilitated by the manufacturer-side channel sales and marketing people; partners have limited, if any, access. Adoption of PRM solutions seemed to be even less than with CRM.

Some of the PRM manufacturers such as Salesforce.com, BlueRoads, PurpleWire or Comergent offer channel-specific solutions for manufacturers managing their partners.

Salesforce.com was the last player entering the PRM market by leveraging their CRM system and building a robust PRM system. The two most featured functions are deal registration and lead management. Their salesforce.com website states:

> The leader in on-demand CRM now delivers the market leading partner relationship management (PRM) application, Salesforce PRM. This <u>award-winning product</u> takes channel success to a new level with breakthrough ease-of-use to help you rapidly increase channel revenue through your partners. And it is fully integrated with Salesforce SFA to provide complete visibility to help you manage your company's direct and indirect sales channels.

While joining late, Salesforce quickly gained market share in PRM and took a leadership position. Elay Cohen, Product Manager PRM inside Salesforce.com, who I had many conversations with, is a thought leader and the driving force behind the PRM initiative.

PurpleWire, another PRM player for instance, offers four modules called "Channel Leads", "Channel Funds", "Channel Incentives" and "Channel Marketer". The PurpleWire website states:

> "channelSUITE™ is a collection of four unique modules that give organizations the ability to automate program operation; establish process and workflow; and monitor partner participation and compliance. channelSUITE™ enables you to move away from the tedious task of juggling program data on spreadsheets to effectively managing automated web-based applications that drive revenue and allow for 24 x 7 access".

Commergent offers more of an e-commerce solution but with strong partner integration. Commergent's website states:

> "The Comergent eBusiness System enables you to coordinate sales and channels, increasing efficiency while improving the customer's experience of your company—no matter how they purchase your products and services. Comergent helps you optimize your partners' and distributors' processes, as well as your own internal sales processes while keeping channel boundaries invisible to customers".

BlueRoads tried another approach. Rather than building a solution for the manufacturers it was the goal to incorporate the partners more actively. The BlueRoads system was built based on our own experience with lead distribution in Computer 200 and Infinigate

When we sent out hundreds and thousands of leads to our partners and requested feedback to know what happened to the leads, we ended up being very frustrated when the expected feedback did not come. None of the incentives we tried worked and the follow-up measures through call centers had been too expensive. It looked like all the marketing initiatives had been for nothing.

At one point, we tried to explore the reason for the lack of feedback. But rather than analyzing all the excuses such as, "Leads are bad," or "No time for follow up," Or "My dog eat my leads," we traced down the path of sales leads from inception all the way down to the salesperson who was contacting the customer and all the way back to where the feedback was supposed to go. The result was eye opening:

The lead was given from "Person 1" in marketing to "Person 2" in channel sales. "Person 2" than divided the leads in buckets and gave them to the regional channel reps. "Person 3" (the channel rep) gave a few leads to "Person 4", who was the key contact from his partner organization. "Person 4" took the lead and gave it to his sales manager, "Person 5". After "Person 5" reviewed the leads and threw 50% away, he gave the rest to his team, where our lead landed at the desk of "Person 6", the sales assistant. "Person 6" took the leads and sent them to her local office in Omaha Nebraska where the office manager "Person 7" received them and gave it to the local salesperson, "Person 8". "Person 8," however, was too busy to follow up, and asked the sales assistant "Person 9" to call the prospect and find out how they could help the prospect. When our channel sales rep (Person 3) was asked about the result of those leads, he needed to ask his contact (Person 4) who obviously had no idea what the status of that lead was. And even if the local sales assistant (Person 8) was willing to provide feedback, it would take weeks to get it back to the manufacturer.

Partners had their own workspace in BlueRoads and were able to select the leads they like or register deals with the respective manufacturer. This was a major step forward. In reviewing the various PRM systems with Partners, BlueRoads was the most advanced based on channel expertise in the company and the fact that procedures were pretty much standardized.

But all PRM systems have two major obstacles to overcome:

a) If partners work with many different manufacturers they had to go into each system separately – even it would be all the same provider. And as projects are based on collaboration with multiple partners nobody can expect the partner to update multiple systems with the same content.

b) If a manufacturer decided to discontinue a relationship with a partner, the partner would lose all their data unless the partner reenters the data in parallel system or spreadsheet.

Those two obstacles plus the cost of implementing PRM made it an enterprise level system where only large manufacturers were able to pay for the system and had the power to enforce partners to sign up.

That said PRM is still an important element in managing partner data, but the hopes that partner would get access to PRM through portals didn't materialize.

But connected to a business network, where all participating parties work similar to a social network and then manufacturers integrate those back into their PRM systems creates a very interesting dynamic. Partners would be able to work in their environment, connect to the network which in turn connects back to PRM.

5.3. Business Networking

This section discusses a new generation of partner/manufacturer collaboration systems that are emerging. Unlike traditional software solutions where a company like a manufacturer purchases a solution that is only for their partners, Business Networking provides an eco system where all players connect to all other player.

Synopsis: Business Networking Systems such as Xeequa are neither channel centric nor manufacturer centric and are not even owned by either part. The name Business Network suggests that it is all about a joint effort to better serve customers in an alliance rather than a one sided partnership. Business Networking Systems helps both sides to actually work closer together by keeping an even greater distance. While it may sound like an oxymoron: supporting the autonomy deepens the relationship.

Xeequa was founded to solve a great problem. One of the great channel proponent, Denise Sangster, who is more known to top level executives as a strategic consultant for global sales strategies and also the one who put up a very successful conference series called "Euro Channels" urged me after some conversations with her clients to solve a problem that exists in channels for ages but is actually a problem for all businesses: Tier down the hierarchies, establish a network and let the natural forces flow through that network. Almost at the same time I had a few conversations with various resellers who all came down to 1 problem: "Whatever PRM system or portal is out there – as long as we have to re-enter all the data it is not going to work for us." It reminded me to a statement from Gregg Kalman, VP Channels at General Networks, who said: "Build a system that can be used by all partners for all manufacturers supporting all the processes." It sounded easy, yet we knew it would be very difficult. So I set down and explored the most important things we would need to make such a solution a reality.

The initial list was simple:

- All partners should work with the systems they have and connect with any other partner (Manufacturer or Channel) whenever they need and want.

- A bridge function would be needed so that channel partners could work with multiple manufacturers simultaneously.

- Collaboration in a way that any partner could share any opportunity with any other partner in a secure and controlled way

- Any channel partner should be able to register a deal with as many manufacturers as they have access to

- Reporting should be available to all participants in a way that it helps improving processes and better manage the alliance.

To create a more detailed specification was the first challenge and immediately the 6th request was created:

- It need to be so simple that everybody can use it without participating in an elaborate education process

In the months to come we drafted a whole new picture of such alliance management software. It was no longer a software deployed by the manufacturer or by the partner, it was something that needed to "sit in the Internet cloud". And rather than creating yet another piece of software that somebody would need to install in parallel to their CRM system we decided we need to leverage existing CRM systems. At the same time a new thing was in the market: social networking. We thought we could leverage that technology but quickly learned that the foundation of social networking is clearly a people to people connection. But we needed connections between people and companies – independent from each other yet very related.

We created an architecture that was the basis for our today's Business Network. It allows to connect companies and their teams as well as supports transactions over that network.

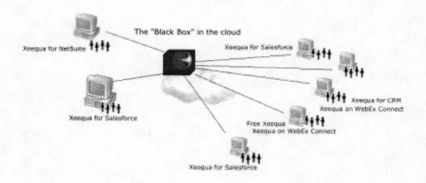

Lead sharing, opportunity management, deal registration and other PRM-like functionality no longer differs from manufacturer to manufacturer with regard to the process flow – yet each manufacturer may have their own terms and conditions. Several of those functions were mentioned throughout the book, where we showed some screenshots of that system.

Some interesting unique features include the alliance relationship map. A map shows the alliances somebody has 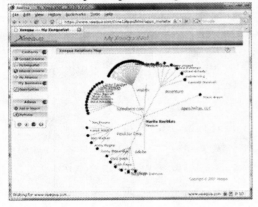 and the users who are part of that alliance. It shows visually very prominent alliances with lot of contacts versus alliances with a very thin contact base. It indicates right away where a relationship should be strengthened or of necessary discontinued.

Operationally the Xeequa approach is very different from classic PRM. Instead of going through an elaborate implementation and deployment process, the system is completely self-service and both partner users and manufacturer users can operate the system and its best practices-based processes immediately. By homogenizing the business processes between manufacturers and partners, partners can adopt a new manufacturer pretty much instantaneously. Likewise, manufacturers who are interested in building a new channel can piggy back on well thought out processes and start their channel initiatives right away. Since the basic functions are for free, manufacturers and partners

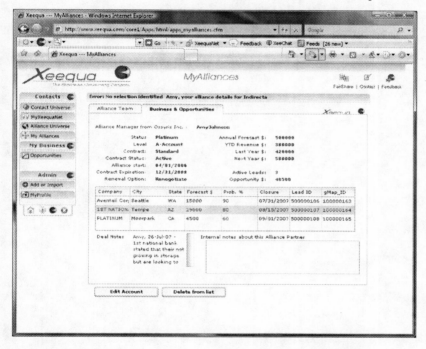

can sign up and start exploring the system immediately.

Another important effect of a networked solution is the ability for all participants to manage THEIR data in THEIR system and not in a system owned by somebody else. The above screenshot shows opportunities somebody is sharing with a partner or manufacturer or both. The data are too critical to not keep track of but at the same time nobody wants to enter them in multiple systems. If an opportunity is managed with 2 manufacturers and a partner peer to make it successful, nobody can expect the partner to feed 4 systems by entering the same content in every system. More information can be found at www.xeequa.com

Summary

Let me summarize what I would consider the most influential aspects of a successful and excellent channel:

A channel sales organization is more complex, more diverse and more demanding than a direct sales force. More people failed to build a successful channel organization than those who succeed for two very simple reasons:

▶ They did not take the channel serious enough

▶ They continued to compete with their partners.

To achieve Channel Excellence:

▶ You do not "try" a channel. Instead you review every aspect of your channel strategy, review it with your partners and execute and improve over several years.

▶ You invest in your channel like you invest in your own team. More than anything else – you make it easy and attractive for your partners to work with you.

▶ You never ever compete with your partners and alliances

▶ You ensure that the channel strategy is deeply embedded in the overall corporate strategy and as such endorsed by CEO and board.

▶ You create a symbiotic relationship between your, and your partners organization that integrates each aspect of your company.

If you like to contribute your experience, like to help others find resources or see the latest in channel development, please visit our wiki and our blog at

http://www.channelexcellence.com

About the Author

Axel Schultze has over 20 years of experience in the IT industry as an entrepreneur with extensive knowledge of channel organizations. He has founded a number of technology companies.

In 1983, he founded Computer 2000, a distributor for personal computer software and hardware. Computer 2000 became the largest high-tech distributor in Europe, the third largest in the world. Mr. Schultze was the driving force for Computer 2000's channel strategy and developed a variety of unique and extremely successful market development strategies. At revenues of $5billion, the company merged with US-based TechData and formed a global IT distribution giant with $12billion in combined annual revenue.

In 1996, Mr. Schultze founded Infinigate AG and grew the revenues from 0 to over $30Million over a four-year period, leveraging a network of over 4000 channel partners in 20 countries. He invented a unique approach to channel management, which became the foundation of BlueRoads, a company he founded in 2001. Leading high tech firms including Avaya, Juniper, Nortel, Hitach Data Systems and others have become BlueRoads customers.

In 2007 he founded Xeequa Corp., a new Business Networking platform, bringing social networking to businesses. Xeequa is the result of his experience with alliance channels and Software as a Service on one side and his networking nature on the other side.

Mr. Schultze started his career as a software developer for General Instruments, where he developed one of the first microprocessor-controlled phone systems, and as an application manager for Rockwell International, where he headed the Microcomputer and Magnetic Bubble Memory Division.

He holds a degree in engineering from the University of Stuttgart and resides in northern California.

Selected Publications, Press

- Author of Magnetic Bubble Memory Technology Published by Markt & Technik

- Author of several channel related articles including:

- "New Lead Management System",

- "Vision 2050", CRN 1

- "Online IPO", Financial Times, New York,

- Channels for the new SaaS industry, white paper

Speaking Engagements

Axel is chairing the <u>SaaS Channel Committee</u> of the SIIA (Software and Information Industry Association).

Speaker at technology events

- Microsoft Channel Partner Events

- Lotus Channel Partner Events

- Internet World Exhibition

- Cebit Future parc

- TV N-TV/CNN

- Bloomberg TV

Endorsements

"When Axel founded C2000 he changed the world in Europe's IT-World both for customers and manufacturers. His visionary approach to facilitate the flow of goods from manufacturer through channel to end user boosted the whole industry. He helped building up the IT-world as we know it today to great extent. He is focused, customer-oriented and - which is not less important- he was always fun to work with." January 23, 2004
Bernd Koch
Former CEO of Schneider & Koch when working with Axel at Computer 2000

"It is clear that Axel is a forward thinking individual that understands selling technology through the channel. He is also a leader and visionary when it comes to delivering Software as a Service. You can't go wrong following Axel as he continues to create new solutions and markets." April 26, 2006
Garth Oliveria
was with a reseller using BlueRoads

"Axel was fundamental in driving C2000 to become the acknowledged leader in IT distribution in Europe. His innovative marketing and sales programs set the standard in creating awareness and professionalism for distributors. I admired his work to such an extent that I eventually joined C2000 myself and later joined Axel in two other companies." January 27, 2004
Steve DeWindt
was with Intel's PCEO division responsible for international sales when working with Axel at Computer 2000

"Axel is one of the most visionary and innovative person I had the opportunity to meet. Axel has original and profound insight into channel business which made Infinigate grow and position itself in the market of Internet distribution companies. His open minded business approach and the freedom he gives his employees was the reason to start working for him. I hardly ever learned so much from any person I worked with and still benefit from these years of learning and gaining experience. I enjoyed working with Axel, could trust and rely on his advice or input at any time." April 3, 2007
Achim B.C. Karpf, *COO/Business Unit Manager, Infinigate AG*
reported to Axel at Infinigate AG

"I have known Axel for 20 years dating back to the mid-80s when we did business together at Computer 2000. He later helped me successfully launch Stac in Germany in the early 1990s. He is a dynamic, innovative marketer. Smart, helpful, friendly and creative are the words I use to describe Axel"
January 25, 2006
Chris Mossing
Former VP Sales, PC Tools.

"Axel is a true innovator and visionary and with his deep channel experience has been able to create not only a product /company but more importantly a new way of doing things in the channel. His hands on and lead-by-example style of management makes him easy to work with as a CEO and easy to learn from as a mentor." November 23, 2005
Puneet Arora, *VP Corporate Sales, Salesforce.com*

"Axel is a highly respected entrepreneur who brings very rich experience and background to channel management. His depth of understanding about business processes and strategic reseller issues helps bridge the gap between theory and what actually works in the real world." November 18, 2005
Michael Lang, *Sales Manager, Oracle*

"Axel's knowledge of the Channels space is unsurpassed in the industry - In my 3 1/2 years working with Blue Roads, during my tenure with Cisco, he was able to clearly articulate channel partner behavior and help design solutions that no other products can address. I would work with Axel again, at the earliest opportunity." November 10, 2005
Gil Ben-Dov
was with Cisco when working with Axel at BlueRoads Corp.

"It's an honor and education working under Axel's leadership. Axel has original and profound insight into channel management and a keen eye for innovation that drives our product vision. As founder, Axel chose the best people, created the right environment, and instilled good values; making BlueRoads a creative and immensely productive workplace where we are proud of what we accomplish together."
November 14, 2005
Christine Diamond
worked indirectly for Axel at BlueRoads Corp.

"Axel is a true visionary of the channel management arena, and over the last several years the BlueRoads product roadmap has perfectly aligned with the evolving needs of companies requiring solutions to optimize channel management performance. Axel is a thought leader in the channel management arena." November 12, 2005
Louis Columbus
was an analyst at AMR research when working with Axel at BlueRoads Corp.

"Axel has boundless energy, entrepreneurial vision and a true passion for advancing the channel. As a leader, I find him to be the perfect combination of visionary, mentor, and champion. Axel is the type of leader that people have confidence in and want to overachieve for, and he is a top-notch human being."
November 10, 2005
Kurt Keesy, *Director of Marketing, BlueRoads*
worked indirectly for Axel at BlueRoads Corp.

"Axel's ability to be one-step ahead of Channel market is unparalleled. He has not only formulated a vision for what solution is needed for Channel customers, but he has been instrumental in ensuring indirect channel customer success for some of the largest corporations in the world. His passion coupled with his energy and experience has cemented BlueRoads as a leader in the Channel CRM market." November 10, 2005
Paul Nagy
reported to Axel at BlueRoads Corp.

"Axel is a dynamic executive with vision and ability to execute that vision. His company/product is solving an age old problem of "how to manage an in-direct channel". I would urge anyone involved in channel management to get to know Axel and his company." November 10, 2005
Doug Barre
Former COO Borland.

"Axel Schultze is truly one of the leaders in our industry and in the channel. His understanding of the channel is superior and is reflected in the software and services that BlueRoads offers. He takes time to understand the business and offered Hitachi a real-world perspective on the channel and making the relationship with partners most effective." November 10, 2005
Charlie Wallace
was responsible for channels at Hitachi Data Systems when working with Axel

"Axel has more practical, real-life experience with indirect channels than anyone I have met during my 25 years of international business development. He has built a highly-effective suite of products that help companies generate a much higher level of revenues from their channel partners." November 10, 2005
Harald Horgen, CEO The York Group

"Axel is one of the most innovating and inspirational person I have got the opportunity to work with. Axel was indeed the driving force while creating a powerful corporate positioning and a International team while transfer Internet2000 to Infinigate, a pure business enabler empowering the Channel and our customers. I strongly recommend Axel as a reliable and focused Manager and Business enabler." November 10, 2005
Jonas Barle
Territory manager, Epicor Sweden

"Axel is an entrepreneur who knows what it takes to succeed: customer focus. His winning team is just as passionate about their customers. They're flexible without loss of effectiveness. They're quick-paced without loss of thoroughness or quality. And they get the job done. They got us the ROI we were so hungry for! And they did so because their leader was as interested in our success as we were." August 19, 2005
Arturo F Muñoz, Director, Global Database Marketing, Hitachi Data Systems, was Axel's client

"It's been my pleasure to work with Axel over the past 2 years. I deal with many CEO's/business leaders, but Axel brings something special to the table; he's driven to solve real business problems and understands his customers' pain. His razor-like focus on customer care ensures he delivers to the highest of expectations. His integrity is solid; he won't let you down."
January 23, 2004
Dawn Block,
was a consultant to Axel at BlueRoads Corp.

"I have known Axel twenty years; initially when he founded Computer 2000 and grew it to be the largest PC products distributor in Europe; attributing to his management skills and expertise of reseller channels and international markets. Axel's successes and visionary abilities enabled him to pull together resources and attract key customers for rapid growth in his businesses." December 8, 2003
Thomas Hong, CEO at Board of CEOs

"I know Axel as an top professional executive and a visionary entrepreneur who has the right touch to enhance business and motivate the people for it. I dealt with him in the EMEA IT business and was impressed by his expertise of the international sales channel." December 21, 2003
Peter De Prins
was with Allaire when working with Axel at Infinigate AG

"I first worked with Axel while he was getting Infinigate started. His existing reputation as a business leader, and someone who understood markets in transformation, attracted Allaire to working with him as a key partner in expanding our business internationally. Over the years, Axel showed a keen understanding of Internet technology and the shifts it would drive in the software business." December 7, 2003
Jeremy Allaire
Founder and CEO of Allaire Software

"I first meet Axel 1983 when he just founded Computer 2000. He is a true visionary and has always been in front of the IT industry in founding the first global IT distributor in Europe, and the first Internet distributor in Europe. He is a brilliant marketing strategist, a strong leader and a great personality. He is very focused in turning ideas into real business." March 26, 2004
Dieter Kondek
CEO Agent VI

"Axel, along with his partners, founded and built one of the most successful computer and software distribution businesses in Europe during the 80's and into the 90's. He is of the highest integrity and has a keen sense of creativity. In fact, we have done business together twice now and are working together on our third project over a 20 year period." January 28, 2004
Chuck Digate, Former CEO Convoge

"I know Axel since the early days of PC productivity software, when productivity actually meant what the word implies!! Computer 2000 became the first partner for Lotus in Germany. Axel was instrumental in winning the Lotus account and building C2000 into the largest European IT distributor. I enjoyed working with him and would have no hesitation in recommending him" January 27, 2004
Irfan Salim
was with Lotus Development when working with Axel at Computer 2000

"I have worked with Axel for twenty five years. Axel is a pioneer and visionary in the field of distribution and channel management. All manufacturers needed Computer 2000 to be their channel partner to penetrate the European market. Axel was particularly insightful determining which industries and products to target for maximum growth and profitability. Gene Hellar CEO, Prima International" December 18, 2003
Gene Hellar
CEO Prima International when working with Axel at Computer 2000

Notes:

Channel Excellence

Notes: